OVERCOMING

THE 4

FAILURES:

Stupid, Lazy, Ugly, & Afraid

DR. ROGER D. SMITH

**Author of *Advice Written on the Back of a Business Card*
and *Becoming the Millionaire Employee***

PRINTED IN THE UNITED STATES OF AMERICA

Visit our web site at www.modelbenders.com

Designed by Adina Cucicov at Flamingo Designs

The Library of Congress has cataloged the paperback edition as follows:

Smith, Roger
Overcoming the 4 Failures: Stupid, Lazy, Ugly, & Afraid.

   Roger Smith.—1st ed.
   1. Career Management   2. Psychology   3. Self-Help
   I. Roger Smith   II. Title

ISBN-13: 978-0-9823040-7-5
ISBN-10: 0-9823040-7-2

Table of Contents

Chapter 1: Living Up to Your Potential 3

Four Failures 6

Building the Wall 7

Who Is Failing? 13

Chapter 2: The Four Failures of Man 19

Where Did These Come From? 21

Destroying Your Worth 25

Stupid 39

Lazy 44

Ugly 49

Afraid 54

Failure-S 59

Chapter 3: Classic Patterns of Failure and Success 61

Measuring Up 64

More Complicated People 69

Real People 73

Graph Yourself 75

Personality Types 76

Chapter 4: Escaping the Past, Elevating the Present 81

Experience 83

Stupid In School 85

Lazy At Work 87

Ugly In Relationships 89

Afraid Of New Ideas 92

Clothed In Failure 94

Changing Patterns, Changing Programming 100

Chapter 5: Stepping on the Scale 105

Adding It Up 113

Chapter 6: Stupid No More 117

What Is Smart? 120

Three Kinds Of Knowledge.........125
Eight Kinds Of Intelligence.........132
Your Talent.........141
Not Conformist.........142
Getting Smarter.........144
Creating a Map.........149
Getting Stupider.........151
Chapter 7: Lazy—Not Today.........153
7 Deadly Sins.........155
Moving From Lazy To Active.........159
Wrapping It Up.........179
Chapter 8: Ugly—Remade.........181
Exchanging Ugly for Attractive.........185
Mental Feng Shui.........198
Rebuilding After the War.........202
Chapter 9: Afraid—Of Nothing.........203
Becoming Bold.........205
Disarming And Disolving Fear.........213
Paradoxical Intention.........216
Chapter 10: Maintaining the New You.........217
Reset.........219
Heroes And Helpers.........225
Talismans.........229
Chapter 11: A Plan to Change.........233
Chapter 12: Tools for Change.........237
Scale.........238
Schedule.........239
Milestone Chart.........240
Goals.........241
Hero Profile.........242
Trait Transplant.........243

CHAPTER

1

Living Up to Your Potential

"*You can grow up to be the President of the United States.*"
"*You can be anything you want to be.*"

These are classic words of encouragement that parents give to their children every day. They are powerful because they are true. We begin life imagining ourselves as the President, an astronaut, a famous athlete, a movie star, a rich businessman. The images of these smiling people are what we see in the media. These are the people that adults look up to. As children, they become our idols, our heroes, and our goals.

As we get older, we discover that the world is so much more diverse, so much richer in variety. Becoming an astronaut is still great, but becoming a rocket engineer also looks great. We begin to see hundreds of different types of people who are all rich in different ways. Some have money. Others lead lives that are noble, personally enriching, dedicated to service, and essential to society. Our brains and our hearts begin to reach out for a special kind of richness that appeals to our unique biology, psychology, and spirituality. As we get older, we find out what the phrase "anything you want to be" really means.

This is natural. It is growth. It is maturity. As we grow in these directions, we pursue goals that our parents never dreamed of. We are normal humans becoming unique, important, and rewarding.

While we are moving toward that goal, at the same time we have to deal with the present. We have to go to school and earn grades. We have to get a job and earn money. We have to pay bills and earn a place in society. While we are doing all of this, we sometimes lose track of the path to our dreams. We forget where we were headed. Sometimes, we remember where we were trying to go, but we lose the path that has taking us there. We abandon it intentionally because it is difficult or distasteful. We abandon it accidentally because we are caught up in the business of daily life. In both cases, we find ourselves headed toward a different goal. Perhaps it is not a goal that we selected, but perhaps it is a goal defined by a company or a social group or a spouse.

Looking back over your life, have you arrived at the goal for which you were aiming? Does the path that you are on lead to the life that you want for yourself? Have you made as much progress as you had hoped by this stage, or at this age, in your life?

Or, have you gotten off the path to your dreams and do not know how to get back on? Have you made much less progress than you had hoped? Do you go to work or school and wonder why the leaders around you do not recognize your potential? Why do they not reward you with the position, money, or respect that your potential calls for?

If you are off the track or are moving slowly down the track, there are four major reasons for this. As you look at the population around you, you see people who are achieving their dreams and people who are not. People who are achieving their dreams have managed to overcome the four major causes of failure in life, career, and relationships. People who are not achieving their dreams have been caught in a net created by one or more of these failures. They struggle forward, but these failures hold them back. These failures hold them tight.

Four Failures

The four major causes of failure are well known. They are not a mystery but they intertwine themselves together in many different forms. They appear as hundreds of different problems, when in fact they are only manifestations of four problems.

Do you know what these failures are? Did you know what they were before you read the title of this book? Do you know which of them has the tightest grip on your heart, your mind, and your future?

Most books present these failures in much more pleasant tones and with more attractive titles. But we want to very clearly get the idea through to you. We want you to remember what these four failures are and to recognize when they have caught you. Our terms are simple, basic, and even brutal.

The four failures are:

STUPID
LAZY
UGLY
AFRAID

When used in our society, all of these words are insults. You do not call your friends these words. They are reserved for people you do not like and with whom you do not want to be associated. In this book, we bring them out into the open and we use them to talk about problems with the most important person in our life—ourselves. We want to define them, expose them, and disarm them. They cannot remain hidden behind niceties. They have to be right out in the open where we can attack them, where we can break them, where we can escape from them.

Building the Wall

Why do these failures continue to influence our behavior, our choices, and our actions? Where do these failures come from? They come from the past. From our childhood, we all grew up through a sequence of thousands of experiences. These experiences changed us as we lived through them.

Let's use the all-American sport as an example of these experiences. We will explain how success in baseball translates into personal strength, and how failure in baseball translates into personal weakness. And baseball is just one example of hundreds of similar experiences that we all go through.

If you chose to play baseball, you were challenged to learn to throw, to catch, to hit, and to run. These are basic to baseball, but not necessarily essential to life. However, if you excelled at all of these skills, then you learned that you had power in your life. You could earn a little bit of respect in your life. You could see yourself as a winner in some small way. In truth, these skills had nothing to do with your bigger life; they were just important in baseball.

Conversely, if you found that you were not good at one or more of these baseball skills, then you began to feel that you were less worthy, less valuable, and less powerful in your life. Other people did not look up to and respect you because of your baseball skills. But you probably mistakenly applied these feelings to your larger, more general life. You began to believe that baseball was equivalent to life. You began to believe that weakness in baseball was equal to weakness in life. Inside, you ranked yourself below the star baseball players— not just when playing the game, but in all aspects of life.

Every day, every week, and every year provides a new challenge—like joining the baseball team. Each experience carries with it a tiny seed of success and power, or disappointment and weakness. Each experience makes you a little bit bigger or a little bit smaller. After thousands of these experiences, a school full of children will have moved themselves to a station in the pecking order of life. They will have defined themselves and will have been defined by society as fitting into a specific niche.

Failures that you experience in childhood come to define what you can and cannot do for the rest of your life. They erect steps and barriers in your mind, in your personality, and in your external behavior. These definitions of failure do not just emerge from baseball and sports; they are picked up from everything that we do, including:

- Academic performance in English, math, and science classes;
- Social performance at parties and group gatherings;
- Outcomes of family arguments;
- Success or embarrassments when dealing with some-one of the opposite sex;
- Accepting or hoping for love from parents, siblings, friends, and acquaintances.

Each of these becomes much more than a one-time experience. Each is a brick in the wall that defines who we are and how we will behave in the future. Each influences who we will be for the rest of our lives. None of them is the final answer. Each is just one brick. Each can be broken and replaced by, or can be reinforced and protected by, a future experience and future outcomes.

None of us make it through these experiences with a perfect batting average. All of us, even the apparently perfect people, accumulate hundreds and thousands of mistakes, failures, and weaknesses in life. We all arrive at our current positions in life with hundreds of scars and tender spots. But we also arrive with hundreds of iron-solid strengths. We all find out where we are really good, really strong, really competent, and really valuable.

You are reading this book because you carry with you one of the four major failures in your life. You may vaguely sense what it is. Or you may have a crystal clear picture of what is wrong. You are here to find out how to overcome that failure, to become strong where you are now weak, and to turn brittle brick into solid iron.

You are reading this book for the same reason that I wrote the book. Because you want to change. Because you want power over your weaknesses and failures. Because you have the will to change and just need the tools to begin the process. The ideas in this book rely on your strength to change. And they are tools that multiply the effectiveness of your strength.

This book is full of pulleys and fulcrums. Physically, you can lift a very small amount of weight straight off the ground. If you are a child, you can lift maybe 20 pounds. An adolescent may lift 60 pounds. An adult may struggle hard enough to life 100 pounds. And an athlete may be able to lift 200 or 300 pounds. When you add tools to the job, the amount of weight that even a small child can lift from the ground greatly increases. Given the right set of pulleys, a child seven or eight years old can lift an entire 2,000-pound car. With tools, a child is stronger than any strong man using only his bare hands.

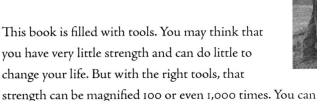

This book is filled with tools. You may think that you have very little strength and can do little to change your life. But with the right tools, that strength can be magnified 100 or even 1,000 times. You can move mountains. It all begins with wanting to, and then equipping yourself with the right tools to allow you to.

The greatest tool in the world is faith. It may be religious faith. It may be personal faith. It may be patriotic faith. But it is faith in the ability of one man, one group, or one god to do anything. As the Biblical verse says:

> *If you have faith as small as a mustard seed, you can say to this mountain, 'Move from here to there' and it will move. Nothing will be impossible for you.*
> **Matthew 17:20**

Faith is the most powerful tool. When coupled with persistence, it can move mountains—and it can certainly move your failures out of your path to let you reach your greatest dreams in life.

This book is about more than faith or belief. It is also about action. You may believe, dream, and imagine a new life for yourself. But you have to take action. You have to change what you do in addition to changing what you believe. In fact, a change in action is often essential if you are going change what you believe. You acquired your current set of beliefs through actions and results. You learned while doing. You are going to acquire a new set of beliefs in the same way—by doing—but by doing something different. You do not get different beliefs by doing the same thing. You only get different beliefs by doing something different.

Apply your own decisions, apply your own actions, and apply the new tools you will have toward doing things differently. This will lead to different outcomes and different beliefs about the world and about yourself.

> *Insanity is doing the same thing over and over, and expecting different results.*
> **Albert Einstein**

> *If you keep on doing what you have been doing, you will keep on getting what you have been getting.*
> **Anonymous**

Who Is Failing?

Carol is a middle-aged woman who has been working for the same company her whole life. She knows how the company works. She knows the customers. She is effective at her job and has been effective at past jobs. But she is faced with a barrier. To be promoted into a senior management position, everyone must have a college degree in business. The executives and the human resources department prefer that this degree be an MBA from a university. But there are a number of roughly equivalent certifications from professional associations and executive management programs, as well as related degrees that will suffice. Carol's barrier is that she already knows everything that she needs to know to hold a senior management position—at least she is convinced that this is true. She has been moving toward this new position for years and has steadfastly refused to pursue the education or certification that she needs to get that job. She is hoping, wishing, believing that the company will waive the rules for her. She believes that her past success and her dedication will carry her over this barrier, and all of this despite the fact that HR and her bosses have made it clear that the business credentials are necessary for her, as they are for everyone else. They believe that such an education is unique, valuable, and essential for these positions. Many of them have taken the same path as Carol and have had their own direct experiences with the company, the job, and the education.

The day comes when that senior management position opens up. HR advertises the position. Carol applies for the position but someone who works for Carol is selected. Carol slammed head-first into the barrier instead of vaulting over it, and she remained at her current lower position while her coworker moved ahead of her. He coworker recognized her own weakness in the face of a promotion and overcame her barrier by earning an MBA. Carol could have done the same thing but chose not to. Finally, after this disappointment, Carol accepts that she has to spend two more years earning the education and then wait for another senior position to open up. And Carol knew all of this for years—she just did not let herself believe it. She chose not to act on it.

Carol is STUPID.

Tim is an outstanding high school athlete. He has played since he could walk and has always had a starring role on both the football and baseball teams at school. He has watched thousands of hours of sports on television, and knows all of the plays and strategies of the professionals. His natural size, strength, and speed usually made it easy for him to outperform his high school friends and opposing teams. He works out and practices with the team just like everyone else, but he never works too hard. The coaches are happy that he helps them win games and championships. But they also feel that he can do better. Every year, visiting college players and coaches talk to Tim about coming to their school. He has participated in their summer camps and they have seen him scrimmage. Though they were impressed with his talent, they encouraged him to work harder in the gym and during practice. They talked about the hard-hitting linemen at the college level and the degree of fitness he will need to make it through an entire season.

But Tim does not listen. He is playing. He is winning. And he is having a great time with his friends. He has a busy social life, lots of events to attend, and lots of people to see. During his college freshman year, Tim makes the starting football team and works hard to contribute to every win. At first, he fails to notice, but each game takes a little more out of him than it did in high school. By mid season, Tim is physically exhausted and worn out. He has minor injuries that nag at him and hold back his performance. He did not build up the stamina necessary to perform well through an entire college season. By the end of the year, Tim's performance is way below that of several teammates who play the same position. He spends more time on the bench and more time being treated by the trainers. At the end of the year, the coaches let Tim know that he is welcome back next year, but that he will not be on the starting lineup and is in danger of losing his spot on the team. When the level of competition increased, Tim failed to step up and increase his own talents and stamina.

Tim is LAZY.

Richard has a PhD in mathematics and is an outstanding design engineer for aircraft engines. He has been leading a number of younger engineers for three years. His team creates very valuable designs for the company. Richard does a lot of the work himself because the younger engineers do the basics but do not seem to understand the real details of aircraft engines. During team meetings, Richard gets so upset that he sometimes explodes and goes on a tirade about how one or two people have dropped the ball and are not carrying their weight. He does not understand why they don't "get it" and why they don't apply themselves to learning more about the field. Richard has gone to the department head and explained the weaknesses of the team. He has pointed out that if he had even one more person like himself, the team could be hugely more productive. When his boss cannot provide another person at that level, Richard is beside himself with frustration. On occasion, he has even gone over his boss' head to the Engineering Director in an effort to get more support for his work.

Richard is dedicated to his own projects. He sees project performance as personal performance. There is no denying that he does some great work. But the people who work for him dread being part of his team. Several have managed to escape to other teams and encourage their friends to follow them. Richard's bosses are tired of being told how to do their jobs and of being accused of not supporting the important work in their departments. Eventually, Richard finds himself working on a "special project" to guide the deliveries of a small subcontractor. He is clearly not in line for an important promotion or headed for an excellent career with the company. Richard has been sidelined and marginalized without being fired.

Richard is UGLY.

Leslie has been playing the violin her entire life. She has been tutored by some of the best teachers in the state. She has performed in school concerts ever since she was four years old. She has rehearsed with the local symphony and played for small parties. But she will not perform at major events. Leslie says she is not as inspired by a large crowd as she is in a smaller and more intimate setting. She is happy to practice with the city symphony anytime that she can. But she will not compete for a permanent chair because that requires that she play in all of their big events and travel to other national events. Leslie is actually a better violinist than some of the people who hold chairs, and she continues to improve.

Leslie will not put herself in a position where she may perform poorly or fail in a big public event. She knows that she makes mistakes and believes that these could all come out during a large, high-pressure performance. Though she loves the violin and loves playing for other people, she cannot let herself get into a leading and visible position.

Leslie is AFRAID.

The people who face one or more of the four major failures of life come from all walks of life. They have every degree of success and failure in their past. In fact, most people are stuck where they are because they embrace the failure. Very seldom are other people pushing failure onto them. We are so obsessed with our own life that it is impossible to police the behavior, the success, and the failure of those around us. Instead, we police ourselves. Each of us is regulated, controlled, and held back more by our own internal beliefs and our own decisions either to take action or to avoid taking action. Changing those beliefs and changing those actions will change the outcome of your entire life, and you will find that there is no external policing body waiting to tell you what you can and cannot do. The world will let you do whatever you choose to do. The first thing you need to do is escape your own reasons for failure.

Men are not prisoners of fate, but only prisoners of their own mind.
Franklin Roosevelt

2

The Four Failures of Man

My daughter is 14 years old. She does very well in school and is a very active dancer. She expects to be able to excel at everything, but without the disappointments of learning and without the setbacks that come in every field. When she gets a bad grade or makes a mistake while dancing, she often bursts out, *"I am just stupid"* or *"I just can't do it and I will never be able to do it."* Neither of these statements is true. They both result from a complex mixture of emotions, memories, and an internal mental conversation that constantly runs in her mind. When she is emotional like this, it is impossible to disentangle all of the emotions and thoughts that have tied themselves into a knot and created the outburst. Perhaps she was lazy in preparing for the event and knows that she should have worked harder. Perhaps she did not understand a concept on a test and knows that she failed to seek out the help she needed to get smarter about it. Perhaps she is afraid that she really has reached the limits of her abilities and will not be able to progress any further. Or perhaps she is so hurt that she is protecting herself from criticism by being ugly to those around her. These are the four major failures that hold everyone back from achieving their goals and dreams.

Emotional statements like *"I am just stupid"* are seldom as simple as they sound. The mental chatter that leads up to these outbursts is even more confusing and less subject to objective analysis. The outbursts wrap up an entire mixture of different emotional and mental ingredients. This makes them almost impossible to diffuse directly. Such statements have to be carefully and consciously taken apart so you can deal individually with each of the ingredients. Taken as a mass, they are unapproachable and undefeatable. In fact, this is exactly the effect that the person hoped for when choosing to behave in this manner.

What is the purpose of this kind of behavior? Self-protection, self-justification, self-satisfaction—basically, the ability of the person to live with himself or herself day in and day out. We can escape from everyone's criticisms, but we can never escape our own minds, our own emotions, and our own self-criticisms.

Where Did These Come From?

This type of self-defense behavior related to our own failures is universal. We see it in everyone, everywhere. Why? How? When did this happen?

Scarcity in a Time of Plenty

Humans and animals have evolved in a world of scarcity. The biggest challenge for most animals, including ancient humans, was the scarcity of food, clothing, and shelter. This meant that, in ancient times, each human spent a majority of his or her time and energy pursuing food, clothing, and shelter. In fact, these people had to be careful not to expend their limited energy frivolously. They had to conserve and use their energy only when it was time to capture or gather more food.

Today, we look at such behavior and we label it laziness. We no longer face a scarcity of food. Most advanced societies have an overabundance of food. But our bodies and minds still seek to conserve energy. In a time of plenty, we still act as if we are in a time of scarcity. People use energy conservation—also known as laziness—as a defense mechanism to preserve life as they know it. Instead, in a time of plenty, they should be exerting much more energy to prosper. This is the time to be an offensive player and not a defensive player.

Are you playing defense when it is time for offense?

Challenged by Our Environment

Animals and humans also begin life with very little knowledge and skills. We begin quite stupid. Then, to survive, the external world pushes us to learn essential skills. It forces us to learn to take care of ourselves and our families. Each of us began life in an environment that demanded certain skills. We developed these skills or we would have been overrun and defeated by the social and natural threats around us.

But the skills that we have developed are far from the limits of our abilities. They form just the minimum set necessary to survive. Some people are born into very challenging circumstances and must learn a very few highly developed skills to survive. Others are born into a relatively secure world and are free to explore many different skills, as no one skill needs extreme development to survive.

This environment leads us to believe that what we have is all that we need, or all that we are capable of. In truth, it is all that we need to remain static, all that we need to remain where we started. But our potential is much, much greater.

Do you want to stay where you are forever?

Disfiguring Effects of Abuse

The people around us and how they treat us also shape us. People have a capacity to care about other people, to develop bonds with other people, and to work together toward larger goals. This tribe mentality has been essential in helping man survive in harsh circumstances and in the face of the extinction of other animals.

Unfortunately, empathy and bonding are traits that other people can destroy in us. Abusive parents, abusive peers, and abusive teachers can eliminate these qualities from us. They can contort the human soul and spirit, making us unable to care about or work with other people. Such people then learn to defend themselves, they learn to distrust others, and they learn to attack before they are attacked. They also learn that they have little personal value in the world. They feel that the world would be just fine, even better, without them in it. The result is a very ugly and destructive personality.

Can you escape your own ugliness?

Allowing Failures to Create Fear

Experiencing joy in life is both a challenge and an accomplishment. And challenges can also lead to failure. Some people experience failure and grow, while others experience failure and whither. The influence, encouragement, and support of other people make a big difference. When left alone with numerous failures, your mind will create fearful stories to explain why "you had no choice." We learn to fear all similar situations. Embracing and personalizing this fear creates a mental script that anticipates failure in every situation.

Each time this person faces a similar situation, his or her mental script starts running. This script triggers the fear response when there is nothing to fear. It explains in great detail why failure will also occur this time. It begins to prepare for failure. It begins to create behaviors and responses that lead to failure.

Though some people's bodies are chemically disposed to produce fear, most of us unconsciously choose to be afraid and we train ourselves to be afraid.

Do you want to be defined by your past failures?

Destroying Your Worth

As a member of the human race, you are one of the most advanced biological being on the face of the earth and the most successful species that has ever existed. Humans have grown from primitive tribes living in caves and hunting for their food like all other animals into a species that can create millions of unique products and manipulate the matter from which the world is made. Though you may feel small compared with history's great thinkers and doers, you remain one of the most amazing creatures to ever exist.

What will you do with all of the talent and abilities that you have? How will you use your package of plentiful ideas that make up the unique person that you are? There are billions of people on the planet. Some use their abilities to accomplish the impossible, and others find it impossible to use their abilities. Which will you become?

The Mind of Man

You are primarily a thinking animal. You were made to use your brain as your primary tool of life, and your brain is larger than many of the greatest thinkers and builders of history. Your brain has 100 billion neurons and each one is connected to 10,000 of its neighboring neurons. It is only 2% of your body mass, but consumes 20% of the oxygen that you inhale and 25% of the glucose that your body creates. Your body is ten times more interested in supporting your brain than any other part of itself. The giraffe takes advantage of its long neck, the elephant of its bulk and tusks, the lion of its teeth and claws. But for the human race, the brain is the primary survival tool.

Each neuron in your brain can fire 100 times per second. This means that every second, your brain can carry out 10 trillion very small operations, and all of them work together to create your thoughts and to guide your actions.

Until the 1950s, scientists believed that the brain was dormant or was turned off during sleep. Today we know that the brain just keeps on working while we are asleep. It is sorting out all of the details of the day, determining what is important, selecting places to store information, and matching new experiences with old ones.

You have little control over how much work your brain does. You can direct it to specific tasks, but you cannot consciously turn it off. With all of this power constantly working inside your head and constantly working in your favor—what will you do with it?

Thomas Edison's Brain

Thomas Edison used his brain to change the world. He created inventions that led to 1,093 patents. Most of these were right around the end of the 19ᵗʰ century when the world was a lot simpler than it is today. Edison completed only three months of formal education, but received extensive homeschooling from his mother and through his own independent reading.

When he was 18, Thomas Edison was a telegraph operator for the railroad and later for Western Union. He asked to be placed on the night shift so he could spend his free time reading and experimenting with the equipment in the office.

Edison owned his brain just like you own your brain. He chose to educate it, explore with it, and invent with it. Initially, he was just indulging his own curiosity. Eventually, this put him in a position to create products that he could use to better his own life and that of his family.

Edison's first patent was for a stock ticker based on the telegraph equipment that he used at his day job at Western Union. He received this patent in 1869 at the age of 22. Though an impressive invention, it did not create wealth or fame. That did not come for eight more years and after many more inventions. In 1877, at the age of 30, Edison introduced the phonograph to the world. The invention was so unique that the general population considered the idea impossible. The invention was so new that it was shocking—and made Edison world famous.

Thomas Edison and you have just about the same kind of brain. Both brains have 10 billion neurons, give or take a few million. Both brains have 10 trillion connections, give or take a billion. Both brains are at the disposal of the human consciousness that we call "me."

What one man can do with his brain, another man can also come close to or exceed. Your brain is capable of much, much more than you have accomplished so far. Will you exercise it like Edison? Will you read and experiment? Both are realistic. Both are achievable. Both are your choice. Or will you remain stupid?

The Body in Motion

An equally amazing body carries your brain around. It is made up of 10 trillion cells that are constantly moving, growing, and changing. Your body is a city of cellular activity. All of these cells form major systems to help you carry out the essential job of living your life.

- The **Musculoskeletal System** includes the bones and muscles that make it possible for you to be mobile and active. Without this system, you would be as stationary as a plant and as formless as a jellyfish.
- The **Cardiovascular System** includes your heart and the veins and arteries throughout your body. This system delivers oxygen and nutrients to all of your muscles, bones, and organs. Without it, there is no life.

+ The **Digestive System** is made up of the organs and glands that can turn food into energy to drive the body. Your body is connected to the world through your mouth.

+ The **Endocrine System** includes the glands that create the hormones that signal your brain and body to function and grow.

+ The **Integumentary System** is the outer layer of your body. It includes your skin, nails, and hair. This system protects you from the outside and keeps the outside out and the inside in.

+ The **Urinary System** gets rid of all of that excess liquid once your body has squeezed the good stuff out of it.

+ The **Lymphatic System** keeps your body healthy and stimulates your immune system.

+ The **Immune System** attacks all of the nasty germs from the outside and the tumors on the inside. This is the police force of the body that keeps order by eliminating the bad guys.

+ The **Respiratory System** brings in the essential oxygen and gasses that are necessary to keep you alive.

+ The **Nervous System** includes the brain and all of the nerves that send information around the body to let it know what is happening on the inside and the outside. This includes most of your senses and the information that they bring in.

+ The **Reproductive System** allows you to make another copy of yourself. This is the Xerox machine of the body, but this machine actually makes other machines just like itself.

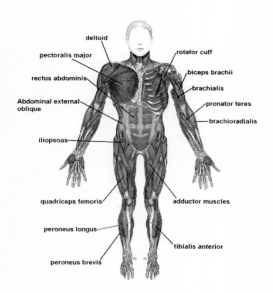

deltoid
pectoralis major
rectus abdominis
Abdominal external
oblique
iliopsoas
quadriceps femoris
peroneus longus
peroneus brevis
rotator cuff
biceps brachii
brachialis
pronator teres
brachioradialis
adductor muscles
tibialis anterior

This long list of functions is amazing. You live inside a machine that is constantly in motion. It is constantly working to keep you alive and safe. This body has the ability to grow, to self-heal, to adapt to the environment, and to carry you anywhere on the planet. You are the owner of one of the most amazing and advanced machines on the planet. It is so amazing that the smartest doctors and scientists still do not know how all of it works. And since you are equipped with such an amazing device, you have the tools necessary to do amazing things in your life.

Michael Phelps' Body

In less than 25 years, Michael Phelps has taught his body to swim faster than any other human body on the planet. He proved this by winning eight gold medals in the 2008 Olympics. Though he was diagnosed with attention-deficit/hyperactivity disorder (ADHD) at a young age, his parents found that swimming was a great outlet for all of his energy.

He used his body instead of his brain to climb to international attention, to excel with his life.

Phelps' body and your body are almost the same. Most people can perform all of the swimming movements that Phelps can perform, though not as rapidly or for as long. But we all possess the ability to be active and strong. Few of us are forced to live a passive and lazy physical life. We share the physical abilities of Michael Phelps more than those of any other species. You are more like a champion swimmer than you are like a sloth or a hibernating bear. Your body is designed to be active, powerful, flexible, and useful in pursuing your goals in life.

Face to the World
Your face to the world is more than just your face. It represents the person behind the face. It is the style of person you choose to use to engage the world in conversation, negotiation, cooperation, and relationship. There are thousands of variations on whom a person appears to be. Psychologists and sociologists have struggled to categorize these, and to create grouping that are manageable but still accurate.

The Myers–Briggs Type Indicator (MBTI) is an extremely popular approach to defining personality types into 16 categories. But there are many others. David Keirsey offers a four-type temperament categorization. Costa and McCrae have popularized the Five Factor Model. There are also the

Four Temperaments based on the ancient four humors of medicine, Type A and B personality theory, the Lithuanian Socionics theory, John Geier's DISC model, and dozens of others.

We will explore some of these in more detail in a later chapter. Each offers some insight into the inner and outer workings of different people. Right now, we are more interested in one basic trait—how ugly or attractive are you to the people around you?

Each of us engages our own unique approach and attitude toward the world every morning when we wake up. We adjust that in unique patterns when we encounter situations and people throughout the day. Many of us believe that we have no control over what we think, how we react, and how we interact with other people. We treat the inner workings of our mind and personality as fixed, programmed at birth, programmed in youth, and impossible to change. We accept that our personality can change as a result of the situations we are in—but, we believe that we have no inner control to make those changes ourselves.

What does it mean to believe that caffeine and loud noises have more control over the inner workings of your brain than your own mind/spirit does? Your mind and spirit reside on the inside, where the personality emanates from, but somehow we believe that this close connection between our mind, spirit, feelings, and behavior is powerless. Instead, we believe that the distant connection to external stimuli that come through our senses is extremely powerful. In some cases, we believe that our reaction to these stimuli is completely uncontrollable, unchangeable, and set in stone.

This creates people who are slaves to their own feelings, who have no control over their behavior, who accept any reaction that is triggered. We believe that some people are programmed to be attractive while others are programmed to be ugly.

Do you accept that you are a slave to your ugliness? If you have ugly traits, are you resigned to keeping them forever? Can it be that you can control everything about your life except your most inner, closely held, and personal reactions to the world?

You may exhibit characteristics of introversion or extroversion. You may make intuitive decisions about the world or you may wait until you have collected a great deal of data. You may guide your life according to conscious decisions or you may be guided by your feelings. You may let the world define itself or you may judge the world by your own standards. These characteristics describe how you are right now. But they do not keep you in a jail cell. They do not define a box in which you must live and reside for your entire life. They are measurement tools, just like a tape measure or a scale. They describe where you are right now. But your actions over time will change where you are. Just as your decisions and behaviors change your height and weight as you get older, they change your personality as you mature. As this occurs, who is controlling the direction you take? Are you in control or are the random forces of the outside world in control?

You can be in control. You can decide what happens to you and how you react to what happens to you.

Oprah Winfrey's Personality

The entire world knows Oprah Winfrey. In fact, we know her so well that the word "Oprah" carries meaning in dozens of countries and languages. She is known from her television show, movies, and charitable work. More than that, she is known for her focus on improving human lives and promoting health, literacy, and self development. This woman's personality has carried her from the underprivileged side of society to a maker and shaper of society.

Anyone with such a positive impact, such a positive attitude, and such a positive outer face must have developed in a very supportive, simulating, and enlightened environment. Right? Wrong!

Oprah was born to a single teenage mother. She grew up poor in Mississippi and Milwaukee. She had her own son at the age of 14 who died tragically as an infant. She lived with her mother as a child and with her father as a teenager. But all of these pressures, disadvantages, and disappointments did not destroy her personality. In fact, these hard times may have made her the strong, positive, encouraging, supportive person that she is. Where did Oprah's amazingly strength and encouraging personality come from? It is not a reflection of the hard times of her early life. She chose her path. She created the person and the personality that now helps the entire world.

Was Oprah able to choose to be attractive or ugly? What power does she have that is above and beyond that of the rest of the people in the world? She was raised in the same environment as millions of others. The difference is that she believed that she had a choice. She believed that she could decide to be attractive rather than ugly.

She chose.

You can choose.

Fear Movies in Our Minds

Your mind hallucinates constantly. These hallucinations are not visual. They do not obscure the real world in the way that hallucinations are depicted on television. Instead, these hallucinations are mental movies that talk to you about every situation you are in, or every situation you imagine and anticipate being in. A hallucination is a picture of how you will behave and perform in that situation.

Our mind creates more words and pictures about the world than what we see with our physical eyes. These words and pictures often create a fear movie that paints a situation that threatens our very being. The fear movie colors a situation as if the outcome will determine the entire course of our lives. The fear movie shows us the worst possible outcome that could happen in every situation. It is not the most likely thing that will happen. It is not what has happened to most other people. It is not what has happened to you in the past. It is much darker and more intimidating than that. But this movie is a lie. We terrify ourselves for no reason.

Fear movies become habitual and they run constantly in our heads, as if we have no control over them. In fact, we have a great deal of control.

Do heroes have these same movies running in their minds? Do the people who save others from burning buildings, invent new computers, make amazing movies, build beautiful skyscrapers, save beached whales, or walk on the moon have these same mental movies of failure? Do they attempt great things while thinking that they will fail? Do they fear to even try? Do heroes fail to see, appreciate, and have confidence in their past successes?

Or... do heroes build movies around their successes? Do their failures lead to mental movies about how the situation could have gone better? Do they turn past failure into future success by creating a positive movie instead of a negative movie? Do they succeed because their own self-created movies show them how to perform successfully and motivate them with the excitement of succeeding?

John Glenn's Spirit

John Glenn dropped out of college to join the Navy after the attack on Pearl Harbor. Though a mundane beginning for a military career, Glenn became a national hero and a symbol of the adventurous spirit of the American people. But before that, he became a Marine Corps pilot and flew 59 combat missions in World War II. Though a very competent pilot, his reputation was built on a propensity to attract antiaircraft fire from enemy ground positions. While flying in the Korean War, Glenn was given the nickname "Magnet Ass" because he attracted so much fire from the ground. On two different occasions, he returned to base with more than 250 holes in his plane from enemy fire. This does not sound like the background of a national hero. Glenn could have focused on the magnet in his behind. He could have played mental movies of his own death from all of this ground fire. He could have become a more conservative pilot or even transferred to a desk job. But that is not what his mental movie told him to do.

After stints as a naval flight instructor, Glenn took a mission to fly the first all-supersonic plane across the United States. Beginning in California, he flew the F8U Crusader to

New York in 3 hours and 23 minutes, moving faster than the speed of sound for almost the entire distance. During the trip, the plane also captured the first panoramic photo of the entire United States.

Though born in a small town in Ohio, dropping out of college, and becoming known as a magnet for enemy fire, Glenn kept moving toward higher goals. He believed that nothing was impossible for him. This led him to pilot the Friendship 7 spacecraft in the first American orbit of the planet. He returned as a national hero and a symbol of America's can-do attitude.

Where was the fear in John Glenn's actions? Was he afraid of enemy fire? Was he afraid of failing in the first all-supersonic flight? Was he afraid of being the first to orbit the planet? Was he afraid to become a U.S. Senator? His actions showed a lack of fear and a decision to be brave, to be bold.

John Glenn was not controlled by fear. He was controlled by bravery and boldness.

Which of these will control you? You feel both of them? Which will you follow?

Stupid

Thomas Hobbs is famous for his statement in the 1600s that the life of primitive man was *"solitary, poor, nasty, brutish and short."* The Neanderthal and Cro-Magnon people that are sometimes called cavemen were slaves to their fears and their lack of understanding of the world. Like little children, they knew very little about the world and had to learn everything by trial and error—often very deadly errors. Unlike children, they had no adults to teach and guide them. Everything was new. Everything was a mystery. Where we have knowledge and science, they had ignorance and superstition. But they had very strong motivation to learn—it is called survival.

For ancient man, ignorance was the norm. But learning was essential if they were to survive the hardships associated with a *"solitary, poor, nasty, brutish and short"* life. They had to learn about weather, nature, animals, and other humans. Everything was a mystery. Superstition, dreams, and the cold mists of fear covered everything in their lives. They were enslaved by ignorance and could turn only to their own experiences for knowledge on how to find food, avoid predators, build shelters, make clothing, and survive diseases.

Though the caveman may epitomize stupidity in modern entertainment, he should also be credited with an extreme motivation to learn as a means of survival.

Stupidity is a primary characteristic of everyone starting a new life, or a new phase of life. The cavemen spanned an entire era of starting anew. Children begin life with no knowledge and no skills. High school and college graduates move into the "real world" with few really practical skills and little real understanding of that world. People changing career fields can be said to be stupid in their new area. New parents know nothing about raising a child. Entrepreneurs starting a new business are ignorant of all of the details and challenges that they must face. Retirees putting their working lives behind them face the prospects of a new and unknown lifestyle ahead of them. Finally, as we approach the end of our lives, we all peer into the unknown realm of death.

In each of these situations, we can be said to be stupid, ignorant, uneducated, and unprepared for the next step in our lives.

In daily conversations, we use the word "stupid" with many different meanings. We could be referring to someone or something that is:

+ Uneducated;
+ Lacking in basic intelligence;
+ Poor in judgment;
+ Inexperienced and lacking exposure to ideas or situations;
+ Poor at planning and executing;
+ Superstitious; or
+ Unwilling to learn.

Each of these is a state that can be addressed and changed. "Stupid" does not have to be permanent. In fact, it was never meant to be permanent. "Stupid" is only an insult to those who live in that state for their entire lives. "Stupid" can be an encouragement to the newcomer to get started with learning, growing, and becoming an expert.

Stupidity is a natural first step in the process of growth. Stupidity is a state in which your opportunities are greatest. You never have the opportunity to learn more than when you know nothing.

Stupidity is a fantastic starting point. But it is a terrible ending point. When you are stupid, you have an opportunity to learn, to start something new, to begin fresh growth, to embark on an adventure.

When you choose to remain stupid, then you are a failure. Stupidity embraced, saved, and treasured is failure embraced and made permanent.

Celebrate the stupidity that is the beginning of growth and opportunity.

Abhor the stupidity that is permanent, disfiguring, and crushing.

Greek God of Stupidity and Foolishness

The Greeks have a god to represent everything in life. Co-alemus in Latin, or Koalemos in Greek, was their god for stupidity and foolishness. His name is derived from the term "hearing foolishness."

The Greeks saw their god of stupidity as being immersed in foolishness. He spent his time listening to words of foolishness, watching acts of foolishness, and participating in acts of foolishness. Everything lighthearted and void of meaning was his meat and potatoes. He immersed himself in the lightest fare of society, knowledge, wisdom, and labor.

Today we say that people "major in minors." This means that they focus all of their efforts, energies, thoughts, and interests on little things that do not matter. The big things escape them or are of no interest. They cannot escape their failures because they are equipped only with the most minor tools, minor knowledge, and minor skills. They are stuck in a rut—specifically, a very small rut.

Getting out of a rut requires changing behavior. It requires acquiring new knowledge and tools. If you are stuck in a small rut, the amount of knowledge and tools necessary to get out is not that large. Small amounts of knowledge can get you out of the "stupidity rut" and start you toward something smarter, something bigger.

You can worry about the medium-sized rut later, after you are out of the small rut.

Plutarch Sees Stupidity

In the second century AD, the philosopher Plutarch described stupid people as "dissolute and bibulous." We do not use those two words much today. But we are very familiar with their connotations in modern society.

Dissolute means that a person lacks restraint and is given to indulgence in things that should be controlled, especially drinking and promiscuous sex. In the modern evolution of our language, we associate this kind of behavior with stupidity. Though there is great tolerance for personal behavior, there is also a common understanding that overindulgence is not the path to prosperity, prominence, and strength in society.

Bibulous is even more outdated. It refers to a fondness for alcoholic beverages. Plutarch seems to have been very hard on drinking as it affects the behavior of men, and as it reduces their contribution to society. He believed that alcoholism was one of the major downfalls of people in the second century and he was not at all shy in pointing this out.

Promiscuity and a fondness for alcohol are not the only expressions of stupid behavior. There are many others. An entire chapter in this book focuses specifically on overcoming stupidity, putting this form of failure behind you, and becoming smart enough to be more successful.

Lazy

The second major failure of man is laziness. Simply not doing anything. Being the person who sits down and does not act, does not think, does not plan, does not contribute.

When people lack food, laziness can be a productive behavior. It can conserve energy for essential and absolutely necessary actions. But when people have an abundance of food, laziness is a wasted opportunity. You are fully fueled, ready to go, able to act—but you refuse to act. Opportunity comes and opportunity goes. And the lazy person sits unmoved through it all.

Most animals appear lazy. Pets spend their lives sleeping and playing. They are taken care of. They simply wait until their owner feeds them, bathes them, and pets them. They have no reason to exert effort except for their own pleasure. Being a kept animal provides all of your needs. But it also saps you of all motivation. When you are kept and cared for, you have no need to exert yourself. You can go from the cradle to the grave leaning on your keeper and your provider. You can spend your life doing just what is necessary to keep the free ride going. You can die without ever exerting yourself.

Laziness comes from two major sources: behavioral programming and personal choice. Some people are raised to believe that they should be kept and cared for by others. They learn to find other people or groups that will provide for them. They turn their lives over to these people and let others determine what their contribution to the world will entail. This works for children, but it is not a strategy for adults to follow during their entire lives.

Others are lazy by personal choice. They have seen the possibilities of their own life and these are unmotivating to them. The potential they see to contribute to the world may seem dull and not worth pursuing. They understand only menial roles for themselves and their energies in the world. Or they may have seen the effort required to make a major and meaningful contribution in the world. The effort appears extreme and beyond their abilities or beyond their tolerance. They decide not to make an effort because doing so appears too hard.

Both behavioral programming and personal choice are sad cases. If you choose to spend your life in laziness then what is the purpose of living at all? What is your contribution to the world? What is your reason for being? What is your excuse for coming into the world?

Laziness is a state of mind and body. You can be lazy in:
+ Action;
+ Thinking;
+ Moving;

+ Planning;
+ Talking; or
+ Organizing.

Each of these is laziness toward a different objective or audience.

Greek Goddess of Sloth

"In the hollow recesses of a deep and rocky cave are set the halls of lazy Sleep and his untroubled dwelling. The threshold is guarded by shady Quiet and dull Forgetful-

ness and torpid Sloth with ever drowsy countenance. Ease and Silence with folded wings sit mute in the forecourt."
Statia, 1st century AD

Statia paints a quiet, drowsy, mindless picture of some of the "sisters of sloth" who create a comfortable cave where they can protect and hide their laziness. As a group, they all support and reinforce each other. They keep out the disruptive forces of industry and hide from the pangs of conscience. In the deep cave, they slumber together and spend eternity doing nothing.

Laziness is not new, nor has it ever been held in high regard. It has always been denigrated and has relied on concealment to remain alive.

Aergia comes from the root word "acedia," which today means apathy. Laziness is not always the root cause of inactivity. It can be motivated, or unmotivated, by apathy. A person who does not care about anything around them can slip into laziness from pure boredom with life, location, and the people around them. This apathy saps the psychological energy of a person. Energy slips away down a deep hole, perhaps into the recesses of the deep and rocky cave of Statia.

You cannot stop being lazy if it is caused by apathy. If you care about nothing around you, then any energy invested in overcoming laziness will itself be drained away by apathy. Apathy calls for a change—a change in location, in vocation, in personal position, in relationships. You cannot overcome apathy from the position that is creating the apathy.

Apathy can cause much more damage than mere laziness. If you do not address it, you can fall into a deep mental depression. You can become lost in a dark mental sea from which you cannot escape.

The term "apathy" was first used to refer to the lack of interest in life exhibited by monks and ascetics who were convinced to live a solitary life. Alone in their minds and often in their outer lives, they lost all interest in their own lives. They lost all direction, purpose, and expectation of contributing to the world.

Leading religions consider laziness to be a sin because it is a refusal to use the talents and gifts that you have been given. When created and invested with life and talent, each person has an obligation to use that talent. A refusal to use the gifts is an insult and a rejection of the purpose of the creator, who gave you those gifts. This is clearly a sin in any theology that teaches that man was created by god and was given purpose by god. The famous list of the *"Seven Deadly Sins"* seems to have begun with the Biblical Proverb (6:16), which lists the *"six things the Lord hateth, and the seventh His soul detesteth"* as:

- ✦ "Haughty eyes
- ✦ A lying tongue
- ✦ Hands that shed innocent blood
- ✦ A heart that devises wicked plots
- ✦ Feet that are swift to run into mischief
- ✦ A deceitful witness that uttereth lies
- ✦ Him that soweth discord among brethren"

Over the centuries, this list has evolved. Older sins were removed from the "seven deadly" list and new ones were added. In 590 AD, Pope Gregory I first coined the actual term, *"The Seven Deadly Sins"* and identified them as:

1. Extravagance (luxuria);
2. Gluttony (gula);
3. Greed (avaritia);
4. Apathy (acedia);

5. Wrath (ira);
6. Envy (invidia); and
7. Pride (superbia).

Laziness is part of apathy, which was later replaced by the term sloth. Some form of laziness has been considered among the worst sins for over 1,400 years. The damage that laziness does to a man, his soul, the people around him, and society in general has been recognized and addressed for centuries.

Solutions to the problem are much more recent.

Ugly

Your face does not make you ugly. Where did that crazy idea ever come from? Maybe Hollywood does not want your face in a movie, but there are thousands or millions people who think your face is outstanding, beautiful, cute, lovely, and many more complimentary characteristics.

Ugly comes from your words and your behavior. You are ugly because you abuse people physically, verbally, or emotionally. You are ugly if you treat yourself like a worthless rag.

Ugly is what you are doing. Ugly is something you can stop doing.

When we are young, we get the idea that there are people with attractive faces and bodies and people who are not attractive. We think that there really is one ideal of what it means to be beautiful. This is a simple and twisted picture of the world. Its very simplicity should be a tip-off that it is an idea created by and for juveniles who cannot see more deeply than the surface of the skin. Unfortunately, because it starts in so many people at such a young age, it is a juvenile idea that persists through life.

One of the biggest failures that men face is being ugly. When you are ugly, other people around you will work to pull you down. They will undermine your work because you are the kind of person who should not get ahead in the world. Conversely, if you are attractive, others will support you and promote your efforts.

Ugly Mind

The ugly mind is filled with destructive, negative, worrying, and hateful thoughts. It is guided by evil to do evil things. The mind directs the actions and words.

Ugly behavior and ugly words do not spring from the body without having first been created and fostered in the mind. Personality is but the outward expression of what is already happening in the mind. To address ugliness, you must start by looking at what is happening in the mind.

We have all heard that, *"Beauty is only skin deep, but ugly is to the bone."* This means that ugliness comes from much deeper within us. It is an outer expression of what his happening all the way down to a person's core.

The bones are the hard centers of our limbs. They are the layer hidden beneath the flesh. Their presence gives form to what we see outwardly. They truly form the framework on which we are built. The size and shape of the bones determine the size and shape of the body.

Ugliness has that same effect on a person. The size and shape of ugliness determines how we look from the outside. It determines how a person is perceived and thought about. Ugliness is the bone upon which our personality is shaped.

Greek Goddess of Ugly

The Greeks did not specify a god to represent the ugliness in the world. But they did have one specifically for strife and discontent. Eris was known for spreading discord among people and for starting wars. She was constantly perceiving some slight or insult against her, and she got revenge by ruining the lives of others.

There is a double lesson in this. If the world is abusing you—real or imagined—then you will become a creator of more ugliness in the world. You will become an Eris. In one story, Eris was not invited to the wedding of Peleus and Thetis because she was so disagreeable to the other gods. This slight very deeply and she decided to exact revenge on the gods. She determined to cause them to be as unhappy as she was. She acquired a golden apple, a highly prized gift among the Greek gods, and threw it among the wedding party. As they gathered around the prize, the gods and goddesses saw inscribed on the apple the words, "to the fairest." Hera, Athena, and Aphrodite all claimed that title as their own, and a fight ensued over who was the fairest among them. According to legend, this rivalry spilled over into the human world and caused the Trojan War, which killed thousands of people.

The ugliness of Eris caused her to interact with others in ways that destroyed harmony and happiness. Her misery caused misery for those around her and it spread from one person to the next.

Ugly brings out the worst in people and it spreads like a disease.

Jekyll and Hyde

The Strange Case of Dr. Jekyll and Mr. Hyde by Robert Louis Stevenson is the classic story of the impact of an ugly person on society. Stevenson brings out the double nature that resides inside all men, and the importance of strengthening the good while disarming the evil. But Mr. Hyde is also the ugly man inside Dr. Jekyll who is waiting to get out. When freed by a powerful elixir, Mr. Hyde controls the body and carries it through the city on a rampage of murder, robbery, and drunken revelry. Hyde spreads fear through the entire city of London. His evil, his ugliness, is so strong that it can affect thousands of other people.

Once Hyde is released, Dr. Jekyll initially enjoys the freedom of his inner demons. He is drunk with the sense of pleasure and abandon that is Mr. Hyde. But as Mr. Hyde becomes more powerful, Dr. Jekyll learns to fear him and seeks ways to keep him bottled up. Mr. Hyde's behavior destroys the lives and serenity of hundreds of people across London. His actions also begin to follow him back to Jekyll's laboratory. Though initially very separate, the lives of Hyde and Jekyll converge, with the evils of one overcoming the good of the other.

Mr. Hyde is the embodiment of man's inner ugliness. He comes out in our treatment of other people and the way we treat ourselves. We are all faced with the decision of Dr. Jekyll of whether to live a positive and constructive life or whether to indulge our inner Hyde and allow it to damage all of the good we have and can do.

Afraid

Fear is the biggest failure in all of history. It leads us to hide inside of ourselves. It makes us avoid people, places, situations, challenges, opportunities, and our greatest accomplishments.

It is said that people fear failure, so they do not try. The fear itself is the failure. If you are controlled by your fear, you have already failed. Doing nothing, doing little, or doing no more than you must is the failure. Working to accomplish

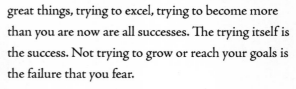

great things, trying to excel, trying to become more than you are now are all successes. The trying itself is the success. Not trying to grow or reach your goals is the failure that you fear.

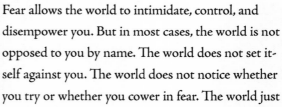

Fear allows the world to intimidate, control, and disempower you. But in most cases, the world is not opposed to you by name. The world does not set itself against you. The world does not notice whether you try or whether you cower in fear. The world just exists and lives. It does not seek to defeat strong people who are trying to grow, change, and better themselves. The world is generally neutral and allows people to pursue and become whatever they are capable of.

When we shut down and stop trying to grow, the world does not take satisfaction at having defeated us or put us in our place. Our failure and disappointment are our own little hell because we are the only ones who notice it or even care.

Fear was meant to be a response to threats and danger. But we have made it much more. It is a response to imagined threats. It is a response to something that exists only in our mind—our mind. Fear has gotten ahead of the stimulus that is supposed to cause it. Like laziness, fear was originally a survival instinct. In the presence of danger, it was supposed to help us stay alive. But most of us live in a very safe environment completely free of danger. We move through each day never facing any threat of physical or financial danger. In an absence of danger, what is to become of the emotion of fear? It does not disappear. Instead, it is transformed into something that tries to protect against our imagination. It makes us flee in the face of imagined dangers. We freeze in our tracks when faced with our own internal picture of some danger that might occur.

How many fears can there be? They are almost without number. Wikipedia gives a list of over one hundred different phobias. These are irrational reactions that are recognized by psychologists.

Phobias Recognized:

Acrophobia · Aerophobia · Agoraphobia · Agraphobia · Aichmophobia ·
Ailurophobia · Algophobia · Anthropophobia · Aphephobia · Apiphobia ·
Aquaphobia · Arachnophobia · Astraphobia · Autophobia · Aviatophobia ·
Aviophobia · Batrachophobia · Bathophobia · Biphobia · Cainophobia ·
Cainotophobia · Cenophobia · Centophobia · Chemophobia · Chiroptophobia ·
Claustrophobia · Contreltophobia · Coulrophobia · Cynophobia · Dentophobia ·
Eisoptrophobia · Emetophobia · Entomophobia · Ephebiphobia · Equinophobia ·
Ergophobia · Erotophobia · Genophobia · Gephyrophobia · Gerascophobia ·
Gerontophobia · Glossophobia · Gymnophobia · Gynophobia · Hamaxophobia ·
Haphophobia · Hapnophobia · Haptephobia · Haptophobia · Heliophobia ·
Hemophobia · Heterophobia · Hexakosioihexekontahexaphobia · Hoplophobia ·
Ichthyophobia · Insectophobia · Keraunophobia · Kymophobia · Lipophobia ·
Megalophobia · Monophobia · Murophobia · Musophobia · Mysophobia ·
Necrophobia · Neophobia · Nomophobia · Nosophobia · Nyctophobia ·
Ochophobia · Odontophobia · Ophidiophobia · Ornithophobia · Osmophobia ·
Panphobia · Paraskavedekatriaphobia · Pediaphobia · Pediophobia · Pedophobia ·
Phagophobia · Phasmophobia · Phonophobia · Photophobia · Psychophobia ·
Pteromechanophobia · Radiophobia · Ranidaphobia · Somniphobia ·
Scopophobia · Scotophobia · Spectrophobia · Suriphobia · Taphophobia ·
Technophobia · Tetraphobia · Thalassophobia · Tokophobia · Tonitrophobia ·
Trichophobia · Triskaidekaphobia · Trypanophobia · Xenophobia · Zoophobia

Most of these pose absolutely no threat to our real life. But thousands of people live every day with one of these phobias. Almost all fears are similar to a phobia—they are irrational, unfounded, crippling, and defeating. But they need not be permanent. There is an escape if you will choose it.

Greek Gods of Fear and Terror

Deimos was the Greek god of fear and terror. His twin-brother was Phobos, who represented the fear during battle that led to panic, flight, and a route by the enemy. The job of these gods was to accompany their father Ares, the god of war, into battle and spread fear wherever he went. Their primary moment of effect was in the face of death. Their power was in getting people to believe that they were going to die.

The mother of Deimos and Phobos was Aphrodite, the goddess of love. Their second area of influence was in relationships. They created a fear of the loss of a loved one. That loss may have been physical, as on the battlefield. But it was also emotional, as in the death of affection that holds two people together.

Fear is an emotion directed at loss. It is meant to separate us from the events that would lessen our lives. It is meant to put distance between us and threatens our physical, financial, and emotional connections. Fear is a mechanism for preventing loss.

When we allow fear to control us, it becomes a mechanism that prevents us from achieving gain. It stops us from trying things that could lead to growth and a better situation.

How does one overcome fear? How do we put it in a box where we can control it? This is what we explore in the chapter on Fear.

The Four Failures of Man

Stupid	Lazy
Not Educated	Does Little
Poorly Educated	Will Not Think
No Valuable Skills	Will Not Take Actions
No Valuable Knowledge	Will Not Move
No Curiosity	Will Not Engage with Other People
Not Learning Every Day	Afraid to Sweat
Not Looking for New Ideas	Will Not Plan
Not Pursuing New Opportunities	Will Not Organize
Ugly	**Afraid**
Personality	Of People
Mind Set	Of the Unknown in Work and Business
Habits	Of Failure
Surroundings—Office, Home, Car	To Try
Personal Appearance—Face, Hair,	Of Appearances
Clothing	Of Peer Pressure
	Of Family Pressure
	To Fail AGAIN
	Of Pain

Failure-S

The four major causes of failure in life do not stand alone. They work together to defeat even the most competent, capable, talented, and powerful people. The human psyche has learned to defend itself in many complex ways, some that are constructive and others that are destructive.

The four failures work together. Laziness passes on opportunities to learn. This leaves people in a state of stupidity. Being stupid about the world makes people fearful. The world is something they do not understand and it scares them. They live in a constant state of fear of the unknown—even though it is an unknown that can be known. If you can over come your laziness and begin moving from stupid to smart, you begin to eliminate your fear as well. Fear also generates ugliness. One of the best defenses against a world that you do not understand is to attack and destroy it. Given your internal fear, you can work to make the external world afraid of you. The four failures link themselves together into an 'S'—the Failure-S. If you allow one of them to exist in your life, it will grow and reinforce the others. But if you kill off one of these, it will weaken all of the others as well.

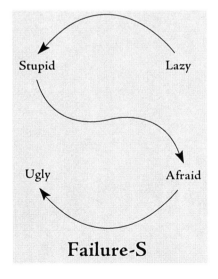

Failure-S

These four failures are a powerful enemy of self, society, humanity, and god. Working together, they create a destructive person and force. People destroy themselves first and then those around them when possible. Overcoming these failures will save both the individual and those around them. It will strengthen society and humanity. Overcoming the four causes of failure is a moral and social imperative.

CHAPTER

3

Classic Patterns of Failure and Success

When Dorothy enters the Land of Oz, she starts on the greatest adventure of her life. From a simple farm in Kansas to a strange yet beautiful world, Dorothy has to learn to cope in an environment that she does not understand. She has to deal with people, relationships, places, and creatures that are new and foreign to her. And, she is

dropped into a situation in which she is put in charge of an important mission and, ultimately, of the lives of her companions. These companions also know a great deal about life's failures. Each is almost a caricature of one particular failure.

Dorothy is uneducated in the ways of the world. She is "Oz Stupid" and is challenged to learn quickly if she is to survive the attentions of the Wicked Witch of the West and get back home.

The Scarecrow is stupid about all things. His lack of knowledge is a great sadness that he does not know how to fix. He is eager to seek out the all-knowing Wizard who can give him brains.

The Tinman has no heart. He is not able to love others. Though a lovable character in the book and movie, he lacks the ability to return that love. He needs someone to show him how to care for others. He needs to overcome his inner emptiness—a shallow form of the ugliness we are describing.

The Lion is a huge coward. He is afraid of everything he sees, hears, and imagines. Fear rules his life, though by nature he is meant to rule the creatures of the forest. He is even afraid of his own voice. He cannot roar because the loud noise scares him. His ability to make a difference in the world is melted away by his own fear.

How does the Wizard cure the inner failures of all of these creatures? He gives them tokens of the trait that they are seeking. In a more ancient language, these are called talismans of the brain, heart, and bravery. The diploma tells the Scarecrow that he is already smart and should use that intelligence. The ticking heart clock tells the Tinman that he has a soft, warm center capable of loving others. The medal for bravery is a testament that the Lion can be as brave as any hero. These items remove their excuses to be stupid, ugly, and afraid. They give each creature permission to be smart, attractive, and brave. In fact, these items are evidence of the trait, and they demand that the creature behave in accordance with the talisman or risk angering the Wizard by denying the powerful gifts that he has given them.

What about the Wizard? What is his failure? He is not stupid. He knows how to solve other people's problems. He is not lazy. He has been running Oz for years. But he is ugly in his dealings with Dorothy and her friends. He scares them and threatens them so they will go away. Why is he ugly to them? At his core, he is afraid. He is afraid that Dorothy and all of Oz will discover that he is a fraud. He is not a Wizard, but a carnival barker from Nebraska. Though the Emerald City has prospered under his rule, though he is respected throughout Oz, though others are happy to allow him to lead, he believes that he is a fraud and unworthy of his position. He is afraid of being found out.

Books and movies create caricatures of real people. They portray our strengths and weaknesses in exaggerated forms. And they provide simplified solutions to all of our problems. They also make the powerful point that there are solutions to all of these problems. They give us an objective view of people who are just like us. They allow us to see our own problems in other people's lives, and to see how these problems can be solved.

We will provide a few caricatures for the four major failures of life. We want to look at a few combinations of stupid, lazy, ugly, and afraid to help you more easily identify these failures in your own life. Later, you will have the opportunity to map yourself to these traits.

Measuring Up

We will take the failure temperature of a number of caricatures that you may recognize. They have names here, and they have names in your life. You may recognize them in your boss, your spouse, your neighbor, a business associate, or a classmate. Feel free to fill in the descriptions and change the names to ones that are meaningful to you.

Each failure's temperature scale runs from 1 to 10. One is the lowest score. It indicates a severe case of a specific failure. Ten is the highest score. It represents a complete ab-

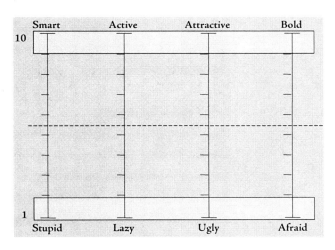

sence of that failure. In fact, it is an abundance of the opposite trait—the traits we strive to create, foster, and grow in ourselves.

Mr. Ford Everything

Ford appears to have been born with a talent for everything. As a child, he led other children and conversed maturely with adults. He earned As in every class without trying very hard. He had the energy to take any class in school, compete in after-school athletics, and hang out with friends in the evenings. He treated everyone warmly and seemed to be the center of conversations and social groups. When summer ended, Ford returned with stories of traveling to Europe, learning whitewater rafting, and playing the guitar.

Ford was smart, active, attractive, and bold. He was the person that others secretly wished they could be. He was a "10" in everything he did. You just knew that both of his parents were also 10s, and he came from a long line of ancestors who were 10s. He seemed to reinforce the idea that royalty really does run in the blood.

Ms. Phyllis Nothing

Phyllis works at the Department of Motor Vehicles. Her job is to handle problems that people had with their driver's licenses, and she created her own system for handling these people. Phyllis got this job soon after dropping out of high school. She spent the summer getting her GED so she could apply for a number of openings in local government. She knew that this kind of work paid pretty well, and allowed her to punch in at 9 and out at 5. She did not have to work late, work overtime, or take work home. As it was a government job, Phyllis also received good benefits and plenty of vacation time.

Phyllis listens to people's problems all day, every day.

"My license did not arrive in the mail."
"The judge took my license, but I have to drive to my family reunion."
"My license says I need glasses, but I can see just fine without them."

What a bunch of complainers. Phyllis does not care about their problems; her answer is always "No!" The best thing to do is tell them that the rules do not allow them to do whatever they want. And if all else fails, she sends them to a different department or agency, just so that they go away.

Phyllis is happy in this job because it allows her to do as much or as little as she wants. But she fears that it cannot support her needs for her whole life. What if she is injured? How will she get another job? What if the state budget cannot afford all of the people on the payroll? What if too many of her customers complain to the boss? She is afraid to lose this job, and she is afraid to leave it. Inside, she has just stopped trying to figure out the world and hopes that it does not notice her.

Mr. Martin Who

There is this guy who works in the cubicle across the aisle from you. He had been there for 10 years. He comes to work early every day and leaves at 5:00 on the dot. He seems to do his work pretty well. What is his name? You have seen him at staff meeting every week for years. You have said "good morning" to him hundreds of time. He has been at every office birthday party.

Martin. You think his name might be Martin. So you step out into the aisle to check his name plate to see if you are right. Yep, that's it. How could you have forgotten what's-his-name?

Martin does not seem to have any big failures. He is relatively smart, certainly not stupid like those people downstairs. He does as much work as anyone else, maybe a little more than a lot of people. He is polite and personable to everyone, but does not seem to have any close friends. During meetings, he presents great information when asked about his work. But he never jumps in to offer his ideas about other projects in the company. He seems to keep what he is thinking to himself.

Martin is a good solid average at everything he does.

Taking the temperature of Ford, Phyllis, and Martin is easy. They are easy stereotypes to whip up. Ford is a 10 at everything. Phyllis is a 1 or 2 at everything. Martin is a 5 or 6 right across the board.

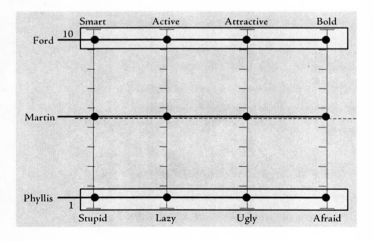

More Complicated People

Most people are much more complicated than Ford, Phyllis, and Martin. Most people have a unique mixture of the four failures. Their graphs tell a different story, one that is more difficult to understand. Very few are overwhelmed by all four failures, like Phyllis. Everyone seems to have something at which they excel. They may fall down in one or two areas, but they make up for it in at least one of the others.

These more complex people are Albert, Robin, Angela, and Chris. They each score high in exactly one of the four areas we are concerned with.

	Ford	Phyllis	Martin	Albert	Robin	Angela	Chris
Stupid/Smart	H	L	M	H	M, L	M, L	M, L
Lazy/Active	H	L	M	M, L	H	M, L	M, L
Ugly/Attractive	H	L	M	M, L	M, L	H	M, L
Afraid/Bold	H	L	M	M, L	M, L	M, L	H

1. Albert and Chris

Albert is brilliant. He even looks like the smartest guy at work. He has more education than everyone and seems to remember everything he has ever read. He will recite information from old reports and recall discussions about projects that happened months ago. Everyone wants to have Albert on their team. He can make things happen.

Luckily, Albert also gets a lot of work done. The bosses know that he is smart, but they also appreciate that he does not spend his time just learning new facts. Albert puts in a full day of work and puts out a good solid amount of product. Luckily, he is also polite and relatively easy to get along with. Albert just has a tendency to correct people in a condescending way if they disagree with his facts.

Albert would go a long way in the company if he could overcome his timidity. In general, he never wants to be in charge. He has declined offers to lead projects, which has cost him at least one promotion. Since he avoids the social circle at work, most people do not know him very well.

Albert has done well and will continue to do well, but his internal fear of other people holds him back.

Chris, on the other hand, wants to be in charge of everything. He jumps up to offer his ideas on absolutely everything. He is eager to be included in any conversation and always thinks that he has the solution to the problem. Unfortunately, what he does not realize is that his solutions are generally terrible. Everyone in the group almost immediately sees that following his advice would make the problem worse.

Though Chris is big on talking, he is not big on acting. He does not love his solutions enough to carry them out on his own. He wants to do part of the work, but needs other people to pick up their share as well. Chris could be a really effective leader if he was just not so stupid and not so lazy.

We have given Albert and Chris each one major strength and one major weakness. The point of this exercise is to illustrate that one strength can make someone valuable at work, respected, and effective. But one weakness can hold them back from the potential to really make a difference and get ahead in their lives. If the other two traits are somewhat mediocre, then such people simply need to improve on their one weakness to really increase their success in life.

Robin and Angela

Robin is an extremely active and busy person. She puts in 50 hours of work each week, and still seems to have the energy to go to the gym every day, ride with the bicycle team on the weekend, support the local food pantry, and attend city council meetings to debate issues in her neighborhood. The amount that she is able to get done astounds everyone around her. In turn, she is astounded at how little everyone else does. She thinks they are lazy and often lets them know that they are generally failing in life. If they are not taking care of their career, their body, their community, and the less fortunate, then they are simply not doing enough.

Working with Robin is usually about constantly rushing since everyone races to keep up with everything she is doing. She can drive a team with her energy alone. When she is talking, it can be a rough ride. You had better put a little armor on your feelings and be ready to defend your position because Robin will engage you like a gladiator on the field of battle.

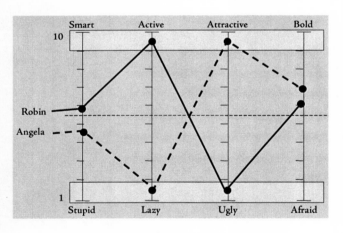

Angela is the belle of the office. She brings goodies for everyone to eat. She has more "best friends" than most people have friends. She knows everyone and everything in the office. She is very supportive of every project that is going on, but not so eager to get tied up with working on any of them. She seems to have a special support role that crosses lots of projects, but no real responsibilities on any one activity.

Angela and Robin are both seen as the heart of the office. Robin is the heart that keeps the blood circulating so everyone can run faster. Angela is the heart that hugs and encourages everyone so they enjoy being there. If Robin just did not hurt so many people in her frenzy, she could run the entire company. Angela is a perfect candidate to be Vice President of Human Resources if she could just start shouldering the extra work that come with an executive position.

Angela and Robin graph with the same high/low imbalance that Albert and Chris had. If they could just improve one area of failure, their lives would be so much more effective and rewarding.

Real People

Now that you have seen a few stereotypes, can you graph specific people that you know at school, work, in the neighborhood, or in a social group? For each of these people, you need to take a guess as to what they are like in the categories

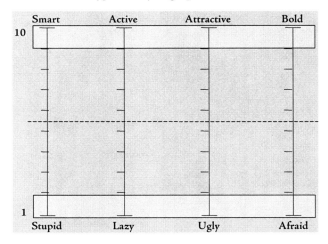

reflecting behavior that you see very little of in them. That is fine. You are just learning to work with these ideas. You are not deciding who will get into the gates of heaven or who will get the next promotion.

Once you have graphed a few of your own acquaintances, try to determine whether their strengths have helped them achieve what they have now. Can you guess at how their failures have hindered them?

Do you see a pattern between the failures and what these people have been able to accomplish for themselves, their families, their communities, and the world around them?

Next, I want you to graph some famous people about whom you have some level of knowledge. You might know something about Thomas Edison, Michael Phelps, Oprah Winfrey, or John Glenn, all of whom we talked about in a previous chapter. Or you might know a completely different set of people, such as Winston Churchill, Barak Obama, Albert Einstein, Walt Disney, Warren Buf-

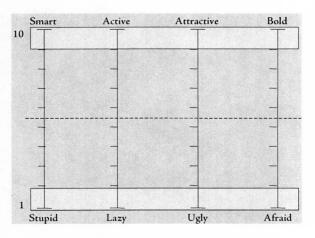

fet, Bill Gates, Steve Jobs, Henry Ford, George Washington, Thomas Jefferson, Abraham Lincoln, or Bono.

Graph some of these people are make notes about how their strengths have helped them get to where they are. You will probably find weaknesses in these great people, and capture those as well. You might notice that their greatest strengths are in the areas in which they chose to focus their career or contribution to society. Great people are not perfect. They have just chosen to pursue areas in which they are really strong.

Graph Yourself

Finally, after all of this practice graphing other people, we want you to graph the person who matters most—yourself. Where do you fall in each of these four scales? In graphing your acquaintances, you learned to make educated guesses, to give others the benefit of the doubt, and to create heroes. Now you can graph what you think about yourself. You can also graph how you think others see

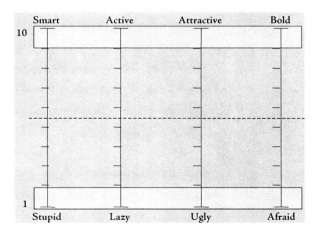

you. Imagine that someone else is graphing you. What would that person say? How would the graph look if it was being drawn by, say, your mother, your boss, your spouse, your children, your neighbors?

If you put all of those lines on the graph, you will really have something to think about.

Personality Types

Many psychological models exist to help explain behavior and personality. Each of these attempts to create categories that typify large groups of people. If you can place yourself into one of these types, then you can understand yourself based on an understanding of the larger group. Doing this is called psychological analysis through stereotyping.

Understanding these personality types can be very useful in understanding yourself. Especially if you believe that you have a unique set of weaknesses or problems. These categories will help you understand that you are one of millions of people who are just like you. You will understand that your problems, aspirations, and approach to life are shared by millions of other people.

Personality types are not the same as the four failures that we have focused this entire book on. But there are relationships between the two sets.

Myers–Briggs

The Myers–Briggs Type Index (MBTI) is one very popular approach to categorizing personalities. Millions of people have taken the test to identify their category. When done as part of a group exercise at school or at work, these categories are useful in enabling teams of people to work together by helping them understand the basic differences between the individuals around them, respecting those differences, and creating assignments and expectations that are aligned with each personality type.

ENFJ	INFJ	INTJ	ENTJ
ENFP	INFP	INTP	ENTP
ESFP	ISFP	ISTP	ESTP
ESFJ	ISFJ	ISTJ	ESTJ

The MBTI has four basic measurements of personality. Each category has two extreme limits that bookend a continuum. The evaluation questions attempt to place each person on this continuum and then assign them to a category.

The four measurements are:

+ Introverted (I) vs. Extroverted (E)
+ Intuitive (N) vs. Sensing (S)
+ Feeling (F) vs. Thinking (T)
+ Perceiving (P) vs. Judging (J)

At the conclusion of the process, each person is assigned a category like ENTJ or ISFP. Details on the behaviors associated with these combined characteristics are provided in

Myers and Briggs' original books and in hundreds of derived works in psychology, management, and relationships.

There is not a one to one correspondence between the four failures and the sixteen personality types. But there are a few clear relationships and similarities.

Introversion and Fear

Someone who is introverted on the MBTI may also be prone to being socially and interpersonally afraid. One of the greatest failures of such a person may come from a lack of comfort in social situations. MBTI suggests that Introverted people are not slaves of their own quiet minds. Instead, they are just more comfortable and energized by quiet reflection and inner thought.

Extroversion and Ugliness

Conversely, extroverts may be so socially aggressive and controlling that they are considered ugly. Their natural tendency to speak, to engage, to lead, and to express themselves may appear to others as an ugly trait meant to control or dismiss the desires of others. Again, MBTI does not say that extroverts have to be abusive or controlling; it merely says that that working with other people energizes them.

Intuitiveness and Laziness

People who are intuitive prefer to make decisions and be guided by their own internal reasoning about situations. Those who are more sensing prefer to collect data and evidence from which to reason. Traditional school systems encourage students to do a great deal of sensing to collect data for decision making. This can lead people to assume that intuitives are lazy because they do not collect data. They do not study the work of others. They are simply being guided by a different principle and a different method of decision making.

Keirsey Temperament Sorter

Myers—Briggs is far from the only theory of categorization of personalities. Keirsey proposes four categories that dominate the types of people. He believes that:

Artisans are observant and pragmatic. Seeking stimulation and virtuosity, they are concerned with making an impact. Their greatest strength is *tactics*. They excel at troubleshooting, agility, and the manipulation of tools, instruments, and equipment.

Guardians are observant and cooperative. Seeking security and belonging, they are concerned with responsibility and duty. Their greatest strength is *logistics*. They excel at organizing, facilitating, checking, and supporting.

Idealists are introspective and cooperative. Seeking meaning and significance, they are concerned with personal growth and finding their own unique identity. Their greatest strength is *diplomacy*. They excel at clarifying, individualizing, unifying, and inspiring.

Rationals are introspective and pragmatic. Seeking mastery and self-control, they are concerned with their own knowledge and competence. Their greatest strength is *strategy*. They excel in any kind of logical investigation such as engineering, conceptualizing, theorizing, and coordinating.

Creating categories that help us understand people has been part of psychology, management, and leadership for centuries, and we can see similarities and differences between the MBTI and the Keirsey Temperament Sorter. More importantly, we see that there are different ways to look at people and the world. Though each method may be useful and accurate to a degree, none is universal and comprehensive.

Readers who would like to compare their strength and failure categories with their personality types are encouraged to investigate a number of the more popular and approachable definitions of personality, such as the:

- Myers–Briggs Type Indicator;
- Keirsey Temperament Sorter;
- DISC Assessment;
- Big Five Personality Traits;
- Minnesota Multiphasic Personality Inventory.

Understanding yourself can be very powerful in accepting, controlling, and changing your behaviors, choices, and successes.

CHAPTER

4

Escaping the Past, Elevating the Present

Gary Hamel says that industry is made up of three kinds of companies. 1) The *rule makers* are the incumbents that dominate the industry today. 2) The *rule takers* are standard participants in the industry that do business the way they are told to. And, 3) the *rule breakers*, who are the revolutionaries who come into the industry and create a new set of rules. These same categories work very well for your personal style and habits. In every organization, family, company, and school, you can find the people who make the rules for how things will happen and who will do what. Then there are the people who accept those rules and do their best to be as successful as possible under the rules created by other people. There are also rule breakers who do not accept these rules. They set up their own rules and attempt to do something completely different. They do not compete in the old game but work to create their own new game.

You will overcome your own failures by becoming a rule breaker. You need not accept the rules that you have been given. You need not measure yourself by what you used to be, what you used to do, or how you used to think. You will put the old rules behind you and define a new set of rules for a game that you can excel at.

Understand that you can't see the end from the beginning. When you get started down this path of change, do not worry if you do not see the final goal that this new path is leading you to. You have a direction, like a compass. But the map to your destination is still cloudy. You can see the next milestone along the path, but the end goal will emerge from the mist as you get closer to it.

When you run a marathon, the end of the race is 26.2 miles away from the beginning. The runners cannot see the finish line. They can only see the markers along the road that point toward the finish line. In a short, 100-meter race, you can see the end from the starting blocks. But life is not a sprint; it is a marathon. Follow the rules of the marathon—just keep following the pointer—and follow your new compass. You will find the end when you get there, not when you start.

Experience

We all rely on our experience to guide our future actions and decisions. But experience is not always the best guide. Experience is valuable only to the degree that the future is similar to the past. If you learned the rules of your life in school, then those rules are not very applicable to your life once you are out of school and working. Similarly, the rules that you created as a novice, young employee are not the ones that will help you when you are doing a much bigger job.

A program runs in your mind. It exhibits itself through your daily behaviors and habits. It comes out in your everyday thoughts, attitudes, and comments. This programming has a great deal to do with who you are and who you will be for the rest of your life.

If the present or future is not the same as the past, then your experience, your old programming, are not good guides for your current life. If you use your old programming, then your present and future will continue to be like your past. That is not growth. That is stagnation.

You are reading this book after years of experience and prior programming that made you who you are and taught you how to behave. All of us learned a little bit every day from the external world about what we "should be," how we "should behave," and what we "should want." By the time we reached adulthood, we were programmed to be a specific person. That person is usually consistent in beliefs, reliable in actions, and predictable in life outcomes. We all may have had dreams, goals, and hopes of what we would like to do and be. But over the years, we were programmed to be something else entirely. If you want to be something different, you have to break your programming. You have to seek out and write a new program for yourself.

Roger Shank, a learning psychologist at USC, points out that the modern school system is still built on the model of the industrial revolution and the factory. It is made to turn out millions of people who behave similarly and have the same knowledge base. It works like a factory designed to mass produce a single product. It is based on the assumption that the professional working world wants an infinite number of these identical people. That is no longer true. The leading world economies need unique, creative, intelligent, self-directed people. Mass production jobs have moved to developing nations like China, Brazil, and India. Those jobs have moved to low-wage countries where the system can create thousands of identical people to do them. The high-end, high-pay jobs that remain in America call for uniqueness, imagination, and self-direction.

Stupid In School

You probably attended a traditional school from about age five to age eighteen. The school was staffed by well-educated teachers and administrators. Its facility was better than that available to your parents or their parents. Experts in their fields designed the curriculum.

School is also a social and intellectual competition for popularity and for grades. Both are a form of acceptance by peers, and by teachers and parents. In this system, some people learn to win approval for their performance in at least one of the major competitive areas.

Each student may have had a liking for one particular subject—English, mathematics, science, history, geography, drama, or music. Some students can master more than one of these subjects. A few students can master all of them, like our friend "Ford Everything" in the previous chapter.

When you mastered one subject as a student, you began
to program yourself to specialize in that area. You learned
that you are "good at math" or "good at English." But you also
learned that you are "bad at science" or "terrible in art." Your
programming began to direct you toward your skills and
away from areas in which you were not so talented.

Realize that all of this happened when you were 8, or 10, or
12, or 14 years old—before the millions of experiences that
you have had in your life. As a child, you saw and did almost
nothing that would become part of your much larger and
longer life. The programming that you got was immature,
just as you were immature as a child. Being "bad at math"
when you were 12 years old did not mean that you would
still be bad at math at ages 25 or 45. Your life background
was completely different at 12 than it is at 45, or your current
age. Your ability to understand ideas is totally different. Your
motivation for excelling in these areas is totally different.

By age 18, you may have been programmed to believe how
smart or dumb you were based on your school experiences.
By the time you were 25, you had developed entirely different
interests and abilities. If you became fascinated by investments
in real estate, stocks, and bonds, then you may have developed
an internal motivation and a need to understand mathematics. You could have been "bad at math" in school because you
had no reason to learn math. Now, you want to understand
interest rates, net present value, rate of return on assets, and

hundreds of other financial ideas to help you make money. Now, you have a lot of motivation to learn math. At this point, you are ready to change your programming and become the best financial mathematician possible.

Forget whatever you learned about yourself in school. You were a child then. You thought like a child. You acted like a child. You made decisions like a child. Today, you are an adult. You have years of different experiences under your belt. You have dozens of different motivations. You have very different priorities. It is time for you to think and act like an adult who needs to and has to control his or her own life.

If stupidity is one of your major failures in life, then think about whether that stupidity has its roots in your experiences in school. If it does, then it is time to escape that programming. You are still using a childhood program. You can replace it with an adult program.

Lazy At Work

We learn if we are lazy when we work at some of our first jobs. Our own actions and the observations of "the boss" begin to tell us whether we can and will work hard. They also tell us whether or not we care about work or prefer to avoid it, goof off, or find some other game to play while we are on the clock.

How did you determine whether or not you are lazy? Was it the job or your boss? Are you lazy because the job is terrible? Or is the job terrible because you are lazy? But what if you are not really lazy at all? What if you learned that you were lazy while working at a job that was the most boring and un-rewarding in the entire town? Does that give you permission to remove the *"I'm lazy"* program from your mind? Does that open the door for you to think of yourself as energetic and motivated in some other area?

If you ask the boss, he **must** say that the job is just fine and the problem is you. He **must** say this because the job will still be there tomorrow. His job as the boss is to find a way for that terrible job to get done. He has little ability to change the job. Even you have little ability to change the job. But you have a huge amount of freedom in changing the job you choose to do. There are dozens, hundreds, or thousands of other jobs around you. You can choose to do one that is much more appealing to your interests.

Should we let our jobs judge and label us? Or should we judge and label the jobs?

When I was in college, I worked at a number of summer jobs. They were all different. They all had positive and nega-tive traits. One was so bad that I had to quit on the first day that I worked. Was I lazy and ungrateful for this job? Or was this just a terrible job—for me? Were the bad jobs fundamentally incompatible with who I was, what I could do, and what interested me?

For most people, laziness goes away when they have a job that interests them. Laziness is usually a mental condition, not a physical one.

Ugly In Relationships

Ugliness is measured in relationships with other people. Family, coworkers, schoolmates, spouses, children, girl-friends, boyfriends, casual acquaintances, store clerks, wait-ers, and salespeople. Do the ties between you and these peo-ple enrich them and enrich you? Or are they taxing, wearing, painful, and repelling?

We all live in an ocean of connections to the people who help us run our lives. None of us lives alone and without connection to or support from other people. One of the most powerful tools and defenses of the human race is its ability to work as a group, to establish larger group goals, and to form the relationships and bonds necessary to pursue those goals. Monkeys have the physical tools necessary to do most of what man can do. But they lack the mental and social ability to work together the way we do. Elephants cluster together to protect themselves from prides of hunt-ing lions. But their group behaviors are simple, basic, and crude compared with those of humans who come together against a common enemy. Humans are more socially active and complex that the other animals. None of us stands alone in our pursuit of life.

> *"No man is an island, entire of itself...any man's death diminishes me, because I am involved in mankind; and therefore never send to know for whom the bell tolls; it tolls for thee."*
> **John Donne, Meditation XVII, 1624**

Even 400 years ago, John Donne could see that all men were interconnected. Since that time, the magnitudes of our group goals and the connections that we all share have increased several fold. In the 1600s, a man might have worked with and depended on one or two dozen people. Today, we can all count hundreds that make up the social web that we are part of. Relationships are essential to being a modern human.

Despite this, each of us has a solitary inner being that seeks to be in total control of life. This being seeks to have its way in all things. We have a desire to be, do, act, and think without the influence of others. We are said to be selfish when that nature is too blatant and dominant, and destructive to our relationships.

Our need for independence and control can often interfere with our need for support and cooperation. We are ugly when we extend our control to other people with no regard or respect for the fact that they have exactly the same need.

If you are ugly to other people or to yourself, you lack the ability to see the value in others or in yourself. You have not learned that every other person has inside of them what you have inside of you. Every other person deserves to be treated with the same respect that you also long to be treated with. In our society, we identify this kind of empathy and consideration as The Golden Rule.

> *"Do unto others as you would have them do unto you."*
> **Jesus of Nazareth, 31AD**

Where does the ugliness that violates this rule come from? Most commonly, it comes from abuse. It grows inside of people as a result of being violated, abused, and negated by other people who have power over them. This abuse may come from parents, schoolmates, coworkers, bosses, or peers. As you endure such abuse, the empathy for other people that naturally lives inside of you begins to rot and mutate. It transforms into resentment. It seeks revenge against those who have hurt you. The inner rot can become your dominant character trait. It can become the primary tool that you use in dealing with outsiders.

If you are ugly to other people, it is generally because you received similar treatment from someone who controlled you in the past. You learned from them to abuse rather than support other people. What you learned may be deep inside of you. But you can unlearn it. Much of what you think of as a depth of ugliness is really just a new layer that you unconsciously renew every day, over and over again. Your mind plays movies of resentment and anger every day to keep this ugliness healthy, strong, and virulent. We now want to uncover methods to stop renewing the ugly so that we can begin to extract that core of ugliness that someone else placed inside of you.

Afraid Of New Ideas

When the Neanderthal man heard a new and strange sound outside of his cave, his first reaction was fear. With little knowledge of the world, his mind knew that it was best to assume that the unknown was dangerous and deadly. His motto could have been, "when in doubt be afraid" or "always fear the unknown." Children start out in life with a very similar instinct. Loud noises and uncomfortable feelings trigger the fear reaction and a call for help. Fear is a primary survival instinct. Without it, humans would walk into unknown situations without caution, only to be eaten by a large carnivore, trampled by a large herbivore, swallowed by a deep pond, crushed by a large snake, frozen in deep snow, or crushed under falling boulders. Your sense of fear helped you live through infancy and childhood to become a mature, functional, and productive part of a larger social group.

But as we grow up, we must overcome our fears and learn to control them. As we learn, as we understand the world in more detail, we understand that patterns exist. We become familiar with many patterns in life and come to recognize the ones that signal danger and the ones that do not. New sensations and new information can be categorized according to these patterns. This means that even if you have never seen or been in a specific situation, you know that it is "like" something that you do understand. This allows you to tag it as safe or dangerous, even though it is really unknown. More experience gives us more patterns, which allows us to quickly and correctly identify similar experiences as either safe or dangerous.

Maturity is the accumulation of knowledge, the creation of personal patterns, and the development of an understanding of how we can function in the world. Maturity is putting fear behind us. Maturity is recognizing what is truly dangerous and what is not. Maturity is pushing back our fear of the unknown to broaden our own lives and the lives of society around us.

Everyone is afraid of situations that are totally unknown. Everyone experiences apprehension when encountering something new. But mature, functional, effective people learn to differentiate truly dangerous things from those that are just unknown.

Mature people develop a confidence in their own abilities to handle situations. This comes from practice, from tackling more and larger challenges. Experience, practice, exploration—all of these give us confidence so that we are not afraid. We conquer our fears a little bit at a time. Making great strides is really about compiling the results of many small experiences and victories.

When fear controls our lives, it holds us in the state of the caveman. It pins us to the back of the cave of our minds. We are terrified to go out and see what is making that strange sound. This is not our destiny. It is not what we were made for. It is not the position to which man has evolved over thousands of generations.

If fear is your primary failure, then you need to experience the small victories that build competence and confidence. We will describe how to do this in later chapters.

Clothed In Failure

The four failures—stupid, lazy, ugly, and afraid—are like a set of clothing. Over the years, you have been given these pieces of clothing and taught to wear them. You have learned that they "look good on you" or that "they complement each other." Inside, you feel a certain degree of comfort wearing your own unique pattern of failures. You may have outstanding intelligence but you wear ugliness along with it, thinking that the two go well together. You may be very attractive personally, but fear keeps you from striking out to discover your real potential. In your own mind's eye, you see attractiveness and fear complimenting each other. You have been told often enough—and you believe—that you have a great personality but that you shouldn't be too aggressive in dealing with other people because "it is not your strength."

As we illustrated in the previous chapter, multiple combinations of strengths and failures exist. There are 16 different combinations if you just score people as either a 10 or a 1 on the scale we introduced. Including the subtle variations of scores within that range gives us 10,000 different variations. Potentially, there are 10,000 different "matching patterns" that "look good on you." As good as any of these look on you, the pattern you wear may not make you happy. You may feel limited, constrained, or imprisoned.

The good news is that, like a set of clothes, you can change the patter. You can try on different patterns. You can copy the styles of other people. Just as people raised in California dress very differently from people raised in Colorado or New York, each of us was raised in a unique social environment that dressed us in the clothes we wear today.

You can take off your old, familiar clothes and try on a new, different, and terrifying set of clothes. Your "old" friends will certainly say that you look different, strange, unnatural, or "not you." But what does your inner voice say about wearing these new clothes? Do they excite you? Do they put a new pep in your step? Do they make it easier for you to pursue your goals and dreams?

When my family and I travel to Europe, we notice that our American style of dress stands out. We notice that people in countries like England and The Netherlands dress in heavier materials and darker colors. There is a rougher, warmer look to their clothes. One day while in The Netherlands, I stood on a rail platform waiting for a train. It was a cold day. I looked around at one hundred locals and nearly all of them had on a heavy black wool coat. Could all of them tell that I was an American just by looking at me? I had on a bright red nylon ski jacket with a bright blue inner lining.

Was I uncomfortable in such a distinctly different outfit? Yes. I was slightly disturbed knowing that I wore a flashing red light that said, *"Look over here at the American!"* But if I had worn that same coat in Colorado during ski season, I would have blended easily into the crowd.

If I moved to The Netherlands, I would change my style of clothing. The change in cultural environment would motivate me to make a big change in my style of dress, and I would purchase a black wool coat to wear in the winter. In the same way, we can all change our behaviors and styles of working with people. However, making that change may be difficult when we are surrounded by people who prefer and expect us to be the person we have always been. These are some of the people who have taught you to be who you are now. You are already who they expect you to be. You can change while staying in the old environment, but you will find it more difficult because forces and people will encourage you not to change.

When told that they can turn failures into strengths, many people will argue quite forcefully that they cannot. They will talk about deep inner programming, nature versus nurture, the biological roots of behavior, and the rigidity of behavior with age. These are real factors that may make such change difficult. But they do not make it impossible. People are among the most adaptive species on the planet. We adapt physically, mentally, and socially. We can learn to live anywhere on earth. People from Florida move to North Dakota and within a year develop a "thick skin" to tolerate the cold. People from dry environments move to the humid South. At first they sweat constantly because their bodies are not accustomed to the external moisture. Eventually, they adapt and become comfortable. If you can do this physically, you can do it with your mind and personality. Humans did not survive and become the dominant species on the planet by being locked into any box, whether physical or mental.

In some ways, your greatest weaknesses are your greatest comforts. Knowing "your place," behaving the way "you are supposed to," and "remembering who you are" create a familiar track through life. They make it unnecessary to consider doing the things that "just are not you." Day after day you live the style of life that you lived the day before. You experience similar sensations, you have familiar conversations, and you express similar behaviors and receive similar responses. Everything is comfortable. If this is exactly what you want from life, then stay put. But if this is preventing you from doing the things that you are eager and hungry to do, then know that you can take off these behaviors—like clothing—and put on a new set that will take you to a new place.

If you just cannot make the change around all of the people who know you the old, familiar way, then move to a new environment. Find a way to move to a place where you can make the change. Find a place to start fresh.

America has a frontier spirit that is unique from that of many other countries. In America, we move from one state to another and from one coast to the other. We seek out new environments and new challenges. In doing so, we escape our own stereotypes and give ourselves the chance to remake who we are. We see the opportunity to try on a new set of clothes.

Not all countries are like this. In many European and Asian countries, people remain very close to their childhood and family roots. They have much less opportunity to redefine themselves and change who they are. They are much more likely to develop their personalities and mindsets in childhood and maintain them for their entire lives. Since they may not change locations for many generations, they have the expected personality and behaviors, as they were expected of their parents and the parents before those. They take on the personality that has been given to their entire family and reinforced for generations. But America is a unique and wonderful place to reinvent yourself. You can exchange your failures for strengths. In America, that is part of our frontier spirit. It is almost part of our constitution:

> *"We hold these truths to be self-evident, that all men are created equal, that they are endowed by their Creator with certain unalienable Rights, that among these are Life, Liberty and the pursuit of Happiness."*
> **United States Declaration of Independence, July 4, 1776**

This book is about the pursuit of happiness. You have the liberty to begin pursuing the happiness that you are looking for.

Changing Patterns, Changing Programming

There are many theories about how the human brain works. How does it learn, store, and recall information, develop speech, create emotions, make connections between different ideas, and carry out hundreds of other functions?

One of the theories is that your brain creates patterns and matches sensory information from the world with previously created patterns that organize everything you have seen, heard, smelled, and touched in the past. Jeff Hawkins believes that your brain uses patterns over and over, all day long, to make your life easier to live.

Jeff suggests a number of simple experiments to help you realize the patterns that are at work every day. When you finish your shower in the morning, take mental note of how you towel off. Your brain and your body have developed a very distinct pattern for drying yourself and your hands work with your subconscious mind to dry your body using the exact same pattern every day. This means that you do not have to consciously think about this action every morning. Instead, you can use your conscious mind to think about something new.

If you want to test the strength of this pattern, make a conscious effort tomorrow to dry off using a different pattern from what you usually use. Move drying from your unconscious to your conscious mind. Your brain and muscles will feel pressure to go back to the familiar pattern. You will feel the strain and concentration needed to do this simple action in a different way. This is just one simple experiment to discover the patterns that are constantly active in your life.

Some people are forced to learn a new pattern for drying after a shower. An injury to a hand or shoulder can make it impossible to dry oneself the old way. What happens next? Initially, they find it just as difficult as you did to use new patterns. Over time, they learn and embed a new pattern. They become trained at and comfortable with a new way of drying themselves.

You can try the same experiment with any of the daily activities that your subconscious mind controls. For example, how do you shave your face or comb your hair? How do you dress and prepare breakfast? All of these activities are pre-programmed in your brain. They are patterns that require little conscious effort.

What does this mean?

The four failures that we are interested in have become patterns in your mind. They make your life easier, like the pattern you use to dry yourself after a shower. They eliminate the need for conscious thought about every little action in your life. These failure patterns are just like the drying, shaving, and dressing patterns that you have developed. You have learned them. But they are not the only patterns that you are capable of following. They can be changed.

Following a mental pattern is easy. It is supposed to be easy. These patterns seem to be an evolution of the brain that makes us more effective and efficient. But all patterns are learned and relearned throughout life. We may relearn a pattern because we move into a new home in a new town. The patterns that helped us function in the old bathroom do not work in the new one. When we move to a new home, the pattern that carried us to work has to be abandoned and a new pattern learned. The pattern that we used when interacting with our old neighbors does not work with our new neighbors. The pattern that made us successful at one company does not work at a new company.

In all of these cases, we create a new pattern. We relearn how to handle a situation. We change to meet the needs of our external circumstances.

Patterns can be changed. Failure patterns can be changed. Patterns that have been active for decades are not permanent. Who we have been does not dictate who we must always be. You consciously change your patterns all the time. You can consciously change your failure patterns.

Patterns are tied to external situations. They are built from and for those situations. So changing a pattern when the external situation has not changed is naturally difficult. The old failure pattern still works in your world. Changing an internal failure pattern is easier if you first change the external environment. This breaks the link between the old pattern and the situations that it was created to handle.

Moving to a new town, getting a new job, or befriending a new set of people are not the only ways to break these connections. We will discuss a number of these later in the book.

Our goal is to change the Failure-S patterns that we discussed in a previous chapter. We want to replace these patterns with Success-S patterns. You can see this pattern in the figure below.

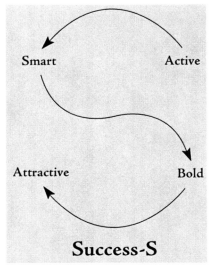

If you change from lazy to active, you become a thinking and doing person. This energy can help you change from stupid to smart. The new knowledge and intelligence that you gain will give you the confidence to shift from afraid to bold. Finally, this new boldness will allow you to exhibit a personality and personal presence that is attractive instead of ugly. This is a Success-S pattern in place of a Failure-S pattern.

CHAPTER

5

Stepping on the Scale

You have seen the graphs of the failures and strengths of different people. We created stereotypes like Ford Everything, Phyllis Nothing, and Martin Who to illustrate this idea.

Then we asked you to guess at the graphs that would represent famous people.

With those as guidelines, we asked you to create a graph of your own strengths and failures. We asked you to do this from your own point of view and also from the point of view of others who know you.

All of this should have helped you talk to yourself about what you do well and what you do poorly. You should have asked and answered some important questions about yourself. But you may have had some difficulty in determining just how strong or weak you are in every area. In this chapter, we present a number of questions to help you bring this out in more detail.

These questions are grouped into explorations of the past, expectations for the future, and experiences of the present. Our memories of the past are sometimes vague and the details have been forgotten. Our feelings about the present are colored by recent emotions and experiences. Our expectations for the future can be exaggerated or muted by our optimism or pessimism. So we include questions across all three of these areas in an attempt to penetrate these distortions.

No matter how many questions we ask and how cleverly we arrange them, you are still the one answering them. They reveal only what you choose to let them reveal. The picture that develops is a combination of what you believe, what you know, what you feel, and what you are willing to admit.
It is time to step up on the scale and see what the needle says.

EXPLORING THE PAST

Everyone has a very rich history that has influenced their perception of the world and their behaviors in that world. We will pose a few questions that attempt to reach into the common background that most people have and bring out some important influencing factors.

Score	-1	0	+1
1. Did you grow up in a traditional family with a father, mother, and siblings?			
2. How would you characterize the relationships between the members of the family?	Fighting	Distant	Close
3. Was there any particular difficulty with any one member of the family? If so how severe would you consider it?	Very Bad	Average	Mild
4. Among your brothers and sisters, are you the oldest, youngest, or in the middle? If you are an only child, then you are the oldest.	Youngest	Middle	Oldest
5. How would you rate your performance in school?	Poor	Average	Good
6. Do you know your overall grade point average in high school?	Less than 2.0	2.0 to 3.0	Higher than 3.0
7. Do you know your overall grade point average in college?	Less than 2.0	2.0 to 3.0	Higher than 3.0
8. In academic classes (these exclude PE, shop, and other action-oriented classes), did you have one area in which you were particularly good?	No	Yes	Several
9. In academic classes, did you have one area where you were very bad?	Several	Yes	No
10. In action-oriented classes (like PE and shop), how would you rate your performance?	Poor	Average	Good
11. What was your attitude toward attending school?	Bad	Bored	Good
12. What was your attitude toward earning grades?	Bad	Average	Good
13. How many close friends did you have in school?	None	Few	Many
14. Did you change your friends as a result of changing schools or towns?	Many Times	Once	Never
15. Were you the bully, the victim, or neither?	Victim	Neither	Bully

EXPLORING THE PAST
Everyone has a very rich history that has influenced their perception of the world and their behaviors in that world. We will pose a few questions that attempt to reach into the common background that most people have and bring out some important influencing factors.

Score	-1	0	+1
16. What did your teachers think of you in general?	Problem	Average	Pet
17. Did one teacher take a particular interest in you and your performance?	No		Yes
18. Were you held back a grade in school?	Yes		No
19. Did you skip ahead a grade in school?	No		Yes
20. Did you participate in organized sports?	No	One	Several
21. Were you active in your own private physical sports?	No	One	Several
22. How much did you read each week, not counting homework?	Less than 1 hour	1 to 5 hours	More than 5 hours
23. Were you teased and belittled by other students?	Yes	Some	No
24. Were you pleased with your experience with your first job?	No		Yes
25. Did you receive a raise or promotion while in this job?	No	A Little	Yes
26. Have you had multiple jobs?	One Job	Two Jobs	More than Two
27. What did you think of your boss in your first job?	Bad	Average	Good
28. What did your boss think of you?	Bad	Average	Good
29. Are your memories of this job good or bad?	Bad	Mild	Good
30. Are your memories of the people good or bad?	Bad	Average	Good
31. How closely did you work with the superstar on the job?	None	A Little	Closely
Past Total			

EXPERIENCING THE PRESENT

The next set of questions focus on the present. They attempt to capture what is happening to you right now, or at least what you think is happening.

Score	-1	0	+1
1. Right out of bed, what is your general attitude?	Bad	Bland	Good
2. Is your very first thought a positive or negative anticipation about the day?	Negative	Neutral	Positive
3. During sleep are your dreams consistently enjoyable, nightmares, or you don't remember them?	Nightmares	Don't Remember	Enjoyable
4. How much time do you spend reading every day?	Less than 30 minutes	30 to 60 minutes	More than one hour
5. How much time do you spend watching television every day?	Less than 30 minutes or more than 2 hours		About 1 hour
6. How much time do you spend playing computer games every day?	Less than 30 minutes or more than 2 hours		About 1 hour
7. How much time is dedicated to family each week?	Less than 1 hour	1 to 3 hours	More than 3 hours
8. If you keep a "to do" list, what percentage of the items on the list get done every day?	Less than 25%	25 to 75%	More than 75%
9. Do you enjoy or dread being with the people you work with?	Dread	Neither	Enjoy
10. How is your relationship with your boss?	Bad	Average	Good
11. Do you have a good or bad office area to work in?	Bad	Average	Good
12. While relaxing at home, does your brain play back movies of problems or victories?	Problems	Little events	Victories

EXPERIENCING THE PRESENT

The next set of questions focus on the present. They attempt to capture what is happening to you right now, or at least what you think is happening.

Score	-1	0	+1
13. If your brain plays problems, do you arrive at solutions to them?	No	Occasionally	Yes
14. Do you bite your fingernails?	No	Some	Habitually
15. At work, do you dress average, better than average, or worse than average?	Worse	Average	Better
16. Is your car clean, filled with clutter, or filled with trash?	Trash	Clutter	Clean
17. Do you have a plan to do something new and different this week?	No	Small	Yes
18. Do you spend your evenings alone, with a few friends, or around many people?	Alone	Few	Many
19. Are you aware of the nutritional value of your major meals?	No	A Little	Yes
20. Does your diet provide you with all essential nutrients?	No	Don't Know	Yes
21. Are you taking vitamin supplements?	No		Yes
22. Are you satisfied by your sex life?	No	Some	Yes
23. Are you making plans to quit or give up on something?	Yes		No
Present Total			

EXPECTING THE FUTURE
Finally, we will explore your thoughts and expectations about the future.

Score	-1	0	+1
1. Do you expect exciting things to happen for you in the next year?	No	Maybe	Yes
2. Do you expect exciting things to happen to you in the next five years?	No	Maybe	Yes
3. Do you have a written plan or set of goals for the future?	None	Some	Many
4. Do your plans have timelines?	No	Some	Yes
5. Do you expect to earn more money next year than last year?	Less	Same	More
6. Do you have a stack of books waiting to be read?	No	Few	Many
7. Will you read these within a year?	No	Some	Yes
8. Do you have a plan or goal for your life that you are doing nothing to pursue?	Yes	A Little	No
9. Are you planning to learn a new skill in the next year?	No		Yes
10. Will your job be better in one year than it is now?	No	Maybe	Yes
11. Is your relationship with your spouse or partner getting better each year?	No	Maybe	Yes
12. Do you expect to be healthier next year than you are this year?	No	Maybe	Yes
13. Are you looking forward to a vacation in the next year?	No	Hopefully	Yes
14. Do you have fearful thoughts about death?	Yes	Occasionally	No
15. Do you believe you will have the same health problems that your parents had?	Yes	Maybe	No
16. Are you spiritually active?	No	Some	Yes
17. Are you physically active?	No	Some	Yes
18. Are you mentally active?	No	Some	Yes
19. Are you emotionally active?	No	Some	Yes
20. Will your family become more or less close in the next year?	Less	Same	More
Future Total			

Adding It Up

We know that some of these questions are difficult or even impossible to answer. They are designed to force you to pull your beliefs about each area out of your subconscious and capture the small nugget of belief that you have. We know that you are not certain about many of your answers. Are they true? Are they accurate? But it is more important that in writing down an answer you captured the seed of what you really believe. For now, treat your initial answer as the truth because it is probably truly your perspective in your own mind. Your subconscious works hard to make sense of all of the little facts that it has collected over time. Without your knowledge or your permission, it often uses many pieces of evidence to build and store an internal belief for you. Consciously, you may not have evaluated and accepted that belief, but it is stored in your subconscious and you use it to make decisions and to set your expectations of the future.

We have assigned a negative one (−1) to each of the unfortunate answers, a positive one (+1) to each of the strengthening answers, and a zero to the mundane answers. To arrive at a positive or negative dominance score, take the following steps:

1. Count the number of answers in the negative column. Record this at the bottom of each section (Past, Present, and Future).

2. Count the number of answers in the positive column. Record this at the bottom of each section.

3. In the Life Total table below, subtract the number of negatives from the number of positives and write that number in its appropriate category. If there are more negatives than positives, then this answer should have a minus sign next to it. If there are more positives, then the answer should have a plus sign.

4. Do this for all three sections, Past, Present, and Future and record the answers in the Life Total table below.

5. Now add the positives together and subtract the negatives to arrive at a single positive or negative answer.

The Life Total Table is meant to make clear whether your past, present, or future expectations are the source of your failures or a source of strengths. A positive future is a good sign that you have maintained your optimism and your expectations for making improvements in your life. However, if your future is negative, then you need to work on changing your expectations and attitudes. These contain the power that will pull you forward.

Life Total Table

Past Total	
Present Total	
Future Total	
Grand Total	

The Present Score indicates how you live each day. This should correspond to the strength or weakness that you feel every day. In the following chapters, we will provide behaviors and changes that you can implement to improve both your Present behaviors and your Future expectations.

We all have a Past Experience. We cannot change what has happened. But we can change what we think and feel about that past. If you have a number of negative items in your past, we are going to show you ways to disarm and diffuse your feelings about these.

Each of the approaches we have used to explore your failure areas is just one tool for determining which of the four areas is a strength and which is a failure. None of them has a magical ability to reveal your true inner and outer self. Like psychotherapy, the external person is just there to help you understand yourself. What they know from their experience and training is helpful, but it relies on your own ability to open up and see the inner workings of your own life.

Use all of this information to help you identify your major failure area and make plans to change it.

CHAPTER

6

Stupid No More

Stupid is a state of mind and performance that is relative to society and the people around you. If you put a teenager in a time machine in 1900 and brought him forward to today, he would appear to be very stupid about this modern world. He would not know how to drive a car, control a television, or simply go shopping at the mall.

Similarly, if you put a 21st century teenager in the same time machine and took her back to 1900, she would be equally

stupid. She would not be able to catch and kill a chicken for dinner, milk the cows, or cook dinner in a wood fired stove.

For most people, stupidity has nothing to do with innate ability or intelligence. Rather, it is a state of not trying to lead, not having the opportunity to learn, and not having the motivation to keep learning throughout life. In other words, it is not an issue of *can't*, it is an issue of *won't*.

We have been programmed to believe that our intelligence is determined and measured by our performance in school. That is too simple. As children and teenagers, we have far too many stimuli in our minds to remain focused on boring classes in math, science, and English. What we really learn from a child's school performance is how motivated he or she is to work toward a future goal. With a goal in mind, students can focus their minds, their time, and their efforts to achieve good grades because those translate into a better future. But without such a goal, there is little that is inherently fascinating about the lessons taught in school. Without a goal, it is no surprise that students do not perform well in class, on tests, and with homework. In fact, poor performance should be what we expect to happen in the absence of a larger goal.

But most of us are no longer in school. That phase of our life is behind us, and we have accumulated years of experience in a different kind of life. We have been in relationships, traveled, held jobs, earned paychecks, paid bills, experienced disappointments, and faced hundreds of other challenges. We are a different person now. We understand much better what the world has in store for us. We have a much better feel for how our actions translate into results in our own lives. We see much more clearly how we are in a position to help or disappoint the people who are important to us.

Given this new place and new perspective on life, we all need to return to learning. We need to revisit our opinions about whether we are stupid or smart. We need to identify the kind of knowledge and skill that will help us become the person that we long to be. It is now time to become smart in an area of our own choosing. It is time to escape the flavor of stupidity that leads to disappointment in our life.

What Is Smart?

Scientists, ministers, leaders, and our peers all have their own ideas about what it means to be smart. Where do these ideas of "smart" come from? Why is one kind of knowledge or ability considered valuable while another is not? Who is to say what makes one smart and what does not?

The answer to this question is not arbitrary. It is not correct to believe that being smart in an area of value is determined by how you feel about that area. Many people believe that if you love some field, then knowledge and skill in it is valuable. That is not correct.

The value of specific knowledge and skill comes from real forces in the lives of individuals and society.

Historical Experience

Humans and society have existed for millennia. Anthropologists believe that Homo sapiens (that is us today) split from the Neanderthals about 500,000 years ago. That is half a million years ago, and roughly 25,000 generations of people. Since that time, we as a species have learned a great deal about what it takes to survive and thrive in the world. Being smart is a measure of your ability to survive and thrive. Any skill or knowledge that helps you do this is "smart." Skills and knowledge that do not contribute to this are hobbies and curiosities. They may be pleasurable, entertaining, and comforting, but they are not essential for survival. That makes them second-tier skills that you can pursue after you have addressed surviving and thriving.

Twenty-five thousand generations of your ancestors have made every mistake in the book. They have done everything the right way and everything the wrong way. Those who avoided survival skills did not survive. They perished and the survivors watched them go. Therefore, historical experience in what works and what does not has been captured and passed down from one generation to the next. Learned survival skills have been retained and reinforced. Inborn survival skills have been passed down biologically.

Internal Intuition

Even when we are kept apart from the influences of other people, each of us has an internal sense of what is dangerous and what is effective in the world. We can look at a situation and recognize that it is dangerous. Peering over the edge of the Grand Canyon, no one has to tell you that jumping in is a bad idea. You may have never actually seen anyone jump into such a huge chasm, but you get a tingling sensation in your stomach when you think about the idea. Something inside of you is pulling your "danger" trigger. No one taught you to feel that ticklish stomach. It is your body telling you to be careful, to back up.

We have this sense to varying degrees about everything that we encounter. There is a good/bad feeling about situations and objects in the world. We have an internal scale that tells us something about the world even when we have very little experience with it.

Social Mores

Society has been around for all 500,000 years of existence of the Homo sapiens. During this time, society has developed guidelines about what is acceptable and what is not. Many of these are unspoken and unexplained. There are some things that you "just don't do." Where did these guidelines come from? There is not one single master of all human interaction that lays down a set of rules.

Social mores are an expression of historical experience. They are derived from the collective experiences of millions of people who came before us. They express a set of rules and behaviors that are effective in living with other people at a specific place and time in the universe. Moral principles vary over time and over places. They are not absolute because the world is very diverse. Very crowded societies develop a set of mores about being quiet and not interfering with the lives of those around you. But societies that exist in wide open spaces with few people allow a much louder and personally abrasive behavior to evolve. Each is an expression of what works in that time and place.

Social mores have encoded the experiences of millions of people in similar situations and attempt to guide you toward the most effective types of behaviors.

Economic Needs

Just as individuals and societies learn what works in inter-personal relationships, businesses have learned what works in economic and professional situations. Centuries of business interactions between people and organizations have resulted in millions of successful ventures and millions of failed ventures. Like other parts of society, businesses have learned what kind of knowledge, skills, and behaviors are valuable and functional in the pursuit of economic gain.

Valuable knowledge and skills—also known as "smarts"—have been identified through trial and error. Businesses are structured to accomplish certain goals and have learned about the kinds of people, the sets of skills, and the body of knowledge that make a positive contribution toward those goals.

Therefore, as we attempt to become smart, there is a huge body of experience and encoded clues about what it means to be smart. You do not have to try to figure out what kind of knowledge and skills you should pursue. Millions of people before you have already made every mistake, tried every combination, and discovered every path to success that you are considering. You can just learn from them. You can stand on their shoulders and begin where others have left off. Archimedes was a brilliant mathematician, scientist, and

inventor who lived in the third century BC. He was particularly interested in creating machines that could increase the amount of work that could be done by the men and animals of his time. He created the water screw and understood the principles behind the lever. He is particularly famous for one quote that survived for over 2,200 years. Wise men around the world have cited these words for over two millennia.

"Give me a lever long enough and a fulcrum on which to place it, and I shall move the world."
Archimedes

Knowledge and skills in the areas that we will describe below are your levers. If you find the right place to put them to use, you can move the world through your own efforts. Knowledge and skill multiply your own efforts and make it possible for you to change the world around you. Such contributions are richly rewarded because they create significant value for the rest of society.

Sir Isaac Newton was another genius of history. He lived from 1643 to 1727 and described the principles of universal gravitation, identified the three laws of motion, built the first refracting telescope, and developed a theory of the colors in white light. Finally, he was the co-inventor of the field of calculus, which is fundamental to modern mathematics, physics, and engineering. But when commenting on his immense contributions to science and society, he maintained that:

> "If I have seen further it is only by standing on the shoulders of giants."
> **Isaac Newton**

His amazing accomplishments were made possible by learning about and using the wisdom of other men. He did not feel that he had done everything himself.

To be smart, you will learn what others already know and then use that in your own life; and to improve the lives of other people.

Three Kinds Of Knowledge

Becoming smart is a process of gathering knowledge and developing skills. Knowledge is what you know. Skills are what you are able to do with that knowledge. Knowledge has been defined many different ways by philosophers, scientists, educators, and linguists. One clear way to categorize knowledge is to describe it as declarative, procedural, and causal.

Declarative

When children begin to learn about the world, they learn the names of things. They learn "mommy," "daddy," "tree," "dog," "chair," and thousands more. This kind of knowledge is necessary for communicating with other people. Declarative knowledge allows you to name, categorize, and talk about a subject. That is what children learn first. Being able to say "tree" or "1972 Mustang Mach I with a Winchester engine" is the very beginning of really identifying with something. Naming is not actionable knowledge. It is the first step in beginning to understand the world.

CANNABIS
SATIVA

Many books and movies detail the work of early botanists in discovering new plants and biologists in discovering new animals. Their first action is to give each of these a name. Their second action is to make an attempt to categorize it. They want to be able to refer to it in conversation and to describe it in their writings. To do that, it has to have a name. Categorizing it is an organized form of naming. It then becomes part of a larger, more general group of things that are like it. But the botanist does not know anything more about the plant when he gives it a name than does an illiterate sailor standing next to him observing the same plant. Declarative knowledge is the beginning of understanding, not the end.

Teachers convey declarative knowledge when they teach children the names of the 50 states and their capitols. This information has no meaning on its own. "Boston, Massachusetts" does not tell you anything about the terrain, weather, agriculture, economy, people, population, or activities of the specific place at the center of the nation with the unique label "Boston, Massachusetts." But this kind of labeling is necessary to begin a conversation about living in the North East. With this label, you can start discussing the effect of a

sea port on weather and the economy that can develop near the ocean. Knowing the states and capitols is knowing nothing. But using these names as labels or handles for a much larger body of knowledge is the beginning of becoming smart.

When you learn the names and words associated with your field of study, you begin the process of talking about it and reading about it. But this is different from really understanding it. Many people develop declarative knowledge about a subject and stop there. They can converse about a city, a tree, or an automobile in very shallow terms. They understand many words and can repeat back what they have read about the subject.

When you have learned some of the terms in your field of knowledge, you have just taken the first step in becoming smart. There is still much further to go.

Procedural

After learning the labels for things, you are ready to understand what those things can do. How do they work? Why are they important? How are they valuable? How are they related to other things? What do they mean to you?

Procedural knowledge is an understanding of how things work. It moves from the label "chair" to knowing what it is doing in the living room, specifically in front of the television. We gain procedural knowledge when we learn to sit in a chair and use it as a vantage point from which to watch television, work on a computer, or operate machinery. We begin to understand how it works, not just what it is called.

When you learn about astronomy, you begin with the names of the planets. But you have to move on to how the planets, sun, and moon work together. How do they make up a solar system? How do they orbit? How long is the length of a day or year on a given planet? If you know how the system works, you can figure out the answers to many questions about a system.

Almost everyone knows what a computer is (declarative knowledge). Most of us know how to use the computer (procedural knowledge). But few of us know why the computer works (causal knowledge). A writer needs procedural knowledge about the computer to write a book. A programmer needs procedural knowledge to create software. A gamer needs procedural knowledge to blast aliens invading the earth. But none of these need causal knowledge about why the computer works. To them, the computer is just a tool. The writer may have extensive causal knowledge in literature and history. But he does not need causal knowledge about the computer to do his job.

In a complex world, we all need procedural knowledge about many different things to pursue our craft, trade, or profession. But all of these areas of procedural knowledge are just support for our primary field.

Every office has a procedural expert. She is the one who knows how "the system" works. She knows all of the processes, rules, and official ways that things should get done. She is your go-to person when you need to understand why something is not working as planned. Though most projects and initiatives in the office do not follow the official process, when they get stuck it is usually because some official rule has hooked them and only an appeal to the rule master can get it unstuck. Procedural knowledge is all around us and we each use it extensively. But this is just the middle level. You do not excel just by knowing how things work.

Causal

Understanding why a computer works is a much rarer level of understanding. People who understand "why" a computer works offer a unique, valuable, and profitable level of knowledge and expertise to society. Everyone who uses the computer relies on their contribution.

These people are valuable because when you understand why something works, you are in a position to fix and maintain the item. You can create a new one. You can make improvements to items that already exist. Procedural knowledge allows you to use the work of other people. But it does not allow you to create new things yourself. To create, you must understand why things work the way they do. This understanding allows you to search for variations that will work better. It allows you to combine knowledge from different fields and create something that no one has seen before. You can achieve this level of creativity, invention, and contribution only after you understand why things work the way they do.

So in your quest to become smart, you will begin with declarative knowledge in which you learn the names of things and how to talk about them. Then you will master procedural knowledge about how these things work and how you can use them in your own lives. But you want to press on to a higher level. You want to move all the way to understanding why something works. Once you have achieved this level, you are one of a select few people who is in a position to create from scratch.

Large drug companies have entire teams of people who understand why chemicals work the way they do. Their goal is to use this "why knowledge" to design drugs with very specific effects. In the 21st century, we understand a great deal about "why" things work, but still not everything. Psychologists try to understand why people think and act in certain ways. They do not want to just follow a recipe book about how to treat a patient. Instead, they prefer to understand why their patient is depressed. Once they know why, it is much easier to select an appropriate solution.

As you move from stupid to smart, you will move through these three levels of knowledge. First, what are the names of things in this field? Second, how do these things work? Third, why do they work this way? If you are a child, you learn the names. If you are an Average Joe, you learn how they work. To become an expert, learn why they work that way.

Eight Kinds Of Intelligence

Everyone has an inherent feeling that there are different kinds of intelligence. The student who excels at math often has difficulty in English. The kids who do very well in English proclaim that "they are not math people." Someone who writes computer software for a living is often completely incapable of fixing the lawn mower, but the engineer down the block can fix it in under an hour.

All through life we find people who are excellent at one set of skills but terrible at another. As life progresses, most of us gravitate toward a job, a hobby, and a lifestyle that allows us to spend most of our time in the areas where we have talent, and to minimize the amount of time we spend in our weakest areas.

Many scientists and psychologists have tried to formally categorize different forms of intelligence. Identifying them and naming them (declarative knowledge) is the first step in being able to discuss them and understand how they work. Over the centuries, hundreds of unique schemes have been used to understand intelligence.

Mystics often described intelligence based on the time of year (astrology), the shape of your head (phrenology), the lines on your hand (palmistry), or the lineage of your ancestry (heritage). These appealed to obvious external characteristics as indicators of internal abilities. Today's cognitive scientists still struggle to understand the inner workings of the brain, but do so with less appeal to the mystical.

In 1983, Howard Gardner published his famous book *Frames of Mind*, which described eight different types of intelligence. His reasoning and descriptions were so clear that this framework has been picked up my many others to explain and study human behavior. Gardner's eight categories of intelligence are as follows: Bodily, Interpersonal, Verbal (linguistic), Logical (mathematical), Naturalistic, Intrapersonal, Visual (spatial), and Musical. These have proven very useful in organizing human intelligence and in valuing each of these forms of intelligence.

As you move from stupid to smart, you will need to become strong and intelligent in at least one of these areas. Hopefully, you will achieve a causal understanding that will make you an expert in at least one field.

Bodily-Kinesthetic Intelligence
This area has to do with bodily movement and physiology. People with bodily-kinesthetic intelligence learn better through muscular movement. When they use their body actively in the learning process, they use it to achieve a much higher level of mastery than if they are learning purely with their minds. These people are generally good at physical activities such as sports and dance. They may enjoy acting

or performing, and in general they are good at building and making things. They often learn best by acting physically, rather than by reading or hearing about the material being learned. People with strong bodily-kinesthetic intelligence seem to use what might be termed muscle memory—they remember things through their physical body.

Careers that suit people with this intelligence include athletes, dancers, actors, surgeons, doctors, builders, and soldiers.

Developing this type of intelligence requires practice and participation.

Interpersonal Intelligence

This category excels at interaction with others. People who have high interpersonal intelligence tend to be extroverts. They are sensitive to the moods, feelings, temperaments, and motivations of others. They possess an ability to cooperate with people and work well as part of a group. They communicate effectively and empathize easily with others. They may be either leaders or followers. They typically learn best by working with others and often enjoy discussion and debate.

Careers that suit people with this intelligence include sales, politicians, managers, teachers, and social workers.

You can develop this intelligence by interacting regularly with other people. Put yourself into more challenging situations, tackle larger team problems, and seek to lead larger groups than you are comfortable with.

Verbal-Linguistic Intelligence

People with high verbal-linguistic intelligence display a facility with words and languages, both spoken and written. They are typically good at reading, writing, telling stories, and memorizing words and dates. They often excel in school because the modern form of teaching is aligned with their special form of intelligence. They are very good at reading, taking notes, listening to lectures, and engaging in discussion and debate. They are also frequently skilled at explaining, teaching, oration, and persuasive speaking. People with verbal-linguistic intelligence learn foreign languages very easily as they have high verbal memory and recall, and an ability to understand and manipulate syntax and structure.

This intelligence is highest in writers, lawyers, philosophers, journalists, politicians, poets, and teachers.

To develop this intelligence, you should read everything you can find on the topic you are trying to master. You should also explore tangents. Andrew Hargedon, management professor at the University of Southern California, has illustrated that the most effective people are actively learning and using information from at least two different fields. Taking ideas from one field and applying them in another is a very powerful approach. For example, an electronics engineer may also be personally interested in building architecture. That interest allows him to draw design and pattern ideas from a field that is much older than his own and which evolved from different roots. These ideas may never be available from within the electronics community because they see problems differently. This two pronged approach to expertise is also common in fields that encourage their engineers to earn an MBA degree to complement their technical view of the world.

Logical-Mathematical Intelligence

Logic, abstractions, reasoning, and numbers are central to this form of intelligence. We often assume that people with this intelligence naturally excel in mathematics, chess, computer programming, and other logical or numerical activities. But a more accurate definition places the emphasis on traditional mathematical ability, reasoning capabilities, abstract patterns of recognition, scientific thinking and investigation, and the ability to perform complex calculations. It correlates strongly with traditional concepts of intelligence as expressed on the IQ test.

Many scientists, mathematicians, engineers, doctors, and economists function with this type of intelligence.

Mastering mathematics is not the same as mastering verbal and written skills. Math and logic require active thinking. They require that you solve problems yourself, not just read about other people's solutions. To grow this intelligence, you must solve problems as a form of mental exercise. In school, students good at mathematics excel because they work problems over and over, not because they read other people's solutions to the problems. Benjamin Franklin used to take mathematical problems and literature and rewrite them in his own words. It was his way of understanding what the original author had done.

John von Neumann was one of the geniuses of World War II and the Cold War. He was a leading figure in the Manhattan Project and later defined the basic structure of the modern computer. He had an outstanding mathematical intelligence. But he lacked the confidence to believe that he could make original contributions to mathematics. Several times, he made what he believed was a unique discovery in mathematics, only to learn that someone else had already done that work. It created in this great man's mind the image that he was unable to do truly original work in mathematics. This idea was born from a few experiences that were less that world-shattering. His own expectation of perfection created insecurity around one of his strongest talents. If this can occur in such a brilliant person's mind, it can occur much more easily in our minds.

Naturalistic Intelligence

Some people excel at dealing with nature and nurturing. These people are said to have greater sensitivity to nature and their own place within it. They have the ability to nurture and grow things. They exhibit a greater ease in caring for, taming, and interacting with animals. Recognizing and classifying things are at the core of a naturalist. They must connect a new experience with prior knowledge to truly understand something new.

Naturalists learn best when the subject involves collecting and analyzing information from the natural world. They don't enjoy learning unfamiliar or seemingly useless subjects with little or no connections to nature. These people should learn more while outside and in a kinesthetic way.

Note that the theory behind this intelligence is often criticized, much like spiritual or existential intelligence. It is seen by many as not indicative of intelligence but rather as an interest.

Careers that suit those with this intelligence include scientists, naturalists, conservationists, gardeners, and farmers. Developing your naturalistic intelligence is very similar to developing physical skills. You need to get out into nature and work with it with your own hands. You need the practice of touching and working with plants, animals, and the earth.

Intrapersonal Intelligence

This area focuses on introspective and self-reflective capacities. People strongest in this intelligence are typically introverts and prefer to work alone. They are usually highly self-aware and are capable of understanding their own emotions, goals, and motivations. They often have an affinity for thought-based pursuits such as philosophy. They learn best when allowed to concentrate on a subject by themselves. This intelligence is often associated with a high level of perfectionism.

Careers that suit people with this intelligence include philosophers, psychologists, theologians, writers, entrepreneur, and scientists.

Visual-Spatial Intelligence

This area has to do with vision and spatial judgment. People with strong visual-spatial intelligence are typically very good at visualizing and mentally manipulating objects. People with strong spatial intelligence are often proficient at solving puzzles. They have a strong visual memory and are often artistically inclined. People with visual-spatial intelligence also generally have a very good sense of direction and may have very good hand–eye coordination, although this is normally seen as a characteristic of the bodily-kinesthetic intelligence.

Some critics point out the high correlation between spatial and mathematical abilities. Solving a mathematical problem involves reassuringly manipulating symbols and numbers. Spatial intelligence is involved in visually changing the reality. Although visual-spatial and mathematical intelligences may share certain characteristics, they are easily distinguished by several factors, and many visual learners have strong logical-mathematical intelligence.

Careers that suit people with this intelligence include artists, engineers, and architects.

Developing these skills requires practice. The artist must draw, paint, or sculpt. She may learn from the works of other people, but she must develop her own talent and unique style through practice. The engineer must design and build objects. The architect must draw and model buildings, bridges, shopping spaces, parks, and every other form of their art.

Musical Intelligence

This area has to do with rhythm, music, and hearing. People with a high level of musical-rhythmic intelligence display greater sensitivity to sounds, rhythms, tones, and music. They normally have a good pitch, and are able to sing, play musical instruments, and compose music. Since there is a strong auditory component to this intelligence, people strongest in it may learn best via lecture. In addition, they often use songs or rhythms to learn and memorize information, and may work best with music playing in the background.

Careers that suit people with this intelligence include musicians, singers, conductors, disc jockeys, orators, composers, and sales reps.

The musician can learn a great deal by reading and listing to the works of others. But to develop personal, internal expertise, he must practice his music, singing, conducting, or talking.

Your Talent

As you read through each of these categories, you probably found yourself surprised by some of them. You may recognize people that you know as fitting neatly into one category or a combination of two of them. You might have said, "*Joe is exactly like the visual-spatial description,*" or "*Alice is logical all the way.*" And you probably attached yourself quickly to one or two of the categories. They sounded natural, right, and descriptive of how you work, learn, and have excelled in the past.

Identifying one or two intelligence categories that are right for you should have been very easy. Most people can expect to find themselves in at least two categories, and sometimes in three of them. You also probably quickly identified the ones that are not at all like you.

Once you recognize where your talents and abilities lie, the big question is: Are you working to excel in that area? Does your profession or future goal align with your talents and inclinations? If the answer to these questions is, "*No*" then you are pursuing a difficult path. If your talents are in an area different from the one that you are pursuing, ask yourself "*Why?*" Why are you pursuing something so different from your internal nature? Is it a desire for money? Are you chasing prestige? Are you targeting the jobs and careers that naturally exist where you live? Are you trying to fulfill someone else's dreams that have been imposed on you?

You can develop your intelligence and skills in any of these areas. Some will come easily to you while others will be more difficult. If you insist on going against your nature, just know that you will find the path more difficult than if you align yourself with your talents.

On the other hand, if you pursue your "smartness" in a form of intelligence that matches your natural inclination, you will find it easier to grow smarter and stronger. Your talents will assist you. Your natural interest will motivate you.

Not Conformist

In his 1903 book *Man and Superman*, George Bernard Shaw said:

> "*The reasonable man adapts himself to the world. The unreasonable man insists on adapting the world to himself. All progress depends on the unreasonable man.*"
> **George Bernard Shaw**

Great people use their talents to break the mold of the world around them. They insist that their purpose in life is not to fit in and go along, but to change the world just a little bit. They seek to make the world better than they found it. In the process, they also benefit personally.

Thomas Edison did not accept that all work should be done by candlelight. Instead, he persisted until he perfected a light bulb that was functional and affordable. Henry Ford did not accept that individuals and businesses should settle for transportation via horse and wagon. He saw a world in which individuals had their own automobiles. He believed that automobiles could be made for the masses, not just for the rich. Alexander Fleming applied penicillin to the treatment of infection. He changed the world in a way that has saved millions of lives.

As you become smart, remember to be unreasonable. Remember to form the world to your own ideals. Each of us can contribute to the world by making it different and better. We may influence only one or two other people, or we may influence millions. But it is important to influence someone for the better. Do not settle for "reasonable." The reasonable man lives and dies and no one remembers that he came and went.

The powerful effect that these smart and unreasonable people have on the world is evidence for why it is important to develop your own intelligence. You can make a similar contribution and have a similar impact, even on a smaller scale.

Getting Smarter

Each of the eight types of intelligence listed above calls for a different type of learning and development of expertise. Most of the methods can be inferred from the short description in the category. In most cases, the key is to practice using and developing that form of intelligence every day. Not every week. Not when you can remember. Not on your day off. You need to practice, study, and grow every single day. Some days you will spend an hour. On other days you will have only five minutes. But you should strive to get better every single day.

Learn

In each form of intelligence, you must learn about the tools associated with your field. You must learn the work of the people who came before you. You must learn about the current thoughts and disagreements about the ideas and practices.

You can learn by listening to others. You may do this with courses, apprenticeships, television, reading, recorded lectures, or observation.

You can learn by reading about the tools, history, and practices in the field. The amount of reading material available is more than most people can consume. But the number of really first-class, leading-edge books or articles is much smaller. Your goal is to begin with any material that you can find, and then to move toward the best works in your field. One of the contributions of university professors is that they have spent decades finding the best works in their field and can immediately point you to sources.

You can also learn by observing the world and other people who do what you want to do. You can consciously note how these people do the work and then make an effort to mimic them. Young teenagers typically learn a great deal about a sport by watching it played before being coached in it. Every sport has a number of rules and basic principles of play. Teenagers can learn these through their own trial-and-error, to the frustration of their coaches. Or they can learn a great deal by watching the game played and noticing the rules that are enforced.

Some people resist the advice to learn the history and important practices of their field. They believe that doing so will dampen their own creativity and originality. They believe that they will just learn to conform to the norm, and will lose their ability to be outstanding. A few people in every generation have a natural talent to excel without following in the footsteps of those who mastered the field before them. But in general, this is not how humans function. Most people are effective and creative as a result of learning about what others have done. They take the work that has happened before them and shape it into a unique form. They rely on the work of other people for the inspiration and guidance in creating their own work. Without knowledge what came before them, their "original work" would be primitive, childish, and far beneath the level that can contribute to the world. More than 99% of people excel because they have learned from others. Less than 1% are able to create something entirely from their inner thoughts and talents. Do not be afraid that learning will stifle your creativity. Rather, be afraid that not learning will starve it. Even Isaac Newton had to "stand on the shoulders of giants."

Practice

As you learn, you should practice. You need to develop the talent in your hands, body, voice, and mind. Learning from others will equip you for practice. But it cannot substitute for practice. You must develop your personal ability to do what others have done before you. You must practice until you can imitate them, compete with them, and excel beyond them.

Practice should include mimicry of the best in the field. You should learn to play basketball like Michael Jordan, deliver motivating speeches like Martin Luther King, perform music like Itzacc Perlman, work through mathematics like Albert Einstein, commune with nature and animals like Jane Goodall, and paint like Picasso.

Practice should also include experimentation with your own forms. You should seek to create unique ways to work in your field or to exercise your intelligence. Pablo Picasso and Jackson Pollack both began as traditional artists. They learned to draw and paint masterfully. But over time, they branched off to experiment with their own forms of art. They sought to speak with an original voice, to make a unique contribution to the art world. This comes about only through experimentation. Your first experiment will generally not be accepted or praised. Neither will your second, third, or fourth. It may take one hundred explorations into the unknown before you discover something that is both unique and valuable. It is not easy because the obvious innovations have generally been captured.

Finally, engage in conversation, debate, and socialization around your field of intelligence. Find others who are pursuing this and work with them. You exchange ideas on what you have been doing. You compete to reach certain levels of accomplishments. You critique the work of others and receive critiques on your own work. You team up with other people to create joint works that go beyond what any one person can accomplish.

Evaluate

As you learn and practice your new skills and intelligences, you need to take some time to reflect. You should think about where this is going, how it is improving, what it is lacking, who can help make it better. Reason about whether you are making enough effort. This reasoning will help you improve your practices. It will help identify and eliminate roadblocks that have come up or that you have placed in your own path. This is a conscious observation of your own performance.

You should also consider an unconscious observation of your practices. For generations, people have prayed for understanding and guidance from a higher power. They have asked to be able to overcome their own weaknesses and limitations. The Christian Bible says, *"If you ask, you shall receive."* This is a spiritual principle. It is also a statement of what your mind can contribute unconsciously if you just ask it.

We are so accustomed to the conscious voice and the conscious movie playing in our head all day that we tend to believe that those thoughts are all that our brains are capable of. This is far from true. The conscious thoughts that you notice are just the surface of what your brain is doing all day and all night. The brain builds patterns from everything it sees and hears. Prayer, meditation, and affirmation are requests to the brain to understand some ideas better, to gain knowledge or skill from a source beyond conscious thought. Prayer and meditation may call on assistance from a divine source; they can also call on the deeper thinking parts of your brain to assist your conscious work. Do not shortchange your efforts by relying only on your conscious thoughts and visible physical practices. Call upon the divine and the subconscious to participate as well.

Creating a Map

We have shown you the major forms of intelligence. We have talked about the different levels of knowledge that exist from declarative, to procedural, to causal. We have shown ways to develop each form of intelligence.

You have heard a number of ways to move from stupid to smart. But without organization, these will fade into memory or tie themselves into complexity. You need to create a map, the Stupid-to-Smart Map. This is a plan that reminds you of where you are, where you are headed, and how you plan to get there. Initially, this map may have little data on it because you learn how to get to Smart as you are going there. Let yourself begin with what you have. You will fill in more details as you go.

You may draw this map as a list of goals. It may be a schedule. It may be a geographic map. It may be a series of pictures that motivate you. Whatever form it takes, it should include the following few key items:

1) A Goal with a Date.
2) A Starting Place and Date.
3) Milestones along the Path.
4) Celebrations of Success.

The goal identifies what you are trying to accomplish, where you are trying to go. It is important to put a date on this. You may have an idealistic goal that extends through your entire life. But you should have smaller goals with real ending conditions and the dates by which you will accomplish these. The starting place and date is a commitment that you have begun the journey. It prevents you from thinking that you are still getting ready, still planning, still preparing. You must state when and where you are starting this journey so that you know that you are on the path right now.

Milestones define specific places along the path that are important. These identify progress. The Romans were the first to create milestones to mark places and distances along the Appian Way, the road that was built in 312 BC to connect Rome to Brindisi. The road was essential for commerce, defense, and communication. The milestones let people know

how far they had traversed to their final destination. Your milestones will identify progress toward your goal in the same way.

Milestones give you something to strive for. They create internal stress to keep moving just a little further, just a little faster. Psychologist Daniel Goleman, who popularized Emotional Intelligence and Social Intelligence in his best-selling books, identified that people who have no stress do not move forward. They remain static. Similarly, people who are extremely stressed by many obligations become paralyzed in place and are unable to move forward because of conflicting demands on their time and energy. But a certain average amount of stress is always present in people who are achieving their goals. Milestones are meant to create just enough stress to keep you moving forward. They are meant to stress you to keep trying to do just a little more.

Finally, you must celebrate along the path. Big goals, big accomplishments, and big changes in your life will take a long time. You cannot withhold all celebration and victory for the very end. You must celebrate and enjoy the path you are following. Ralph Waldo Emerson wrote that, *"Life is a journey, not a destination."* You are embarking on a lifelong journey. Will it be a journey that you celebrate or that you endure?

Getting Stupider

Getting stupider is easy and painful. It is easy because you can do it by simply doing nothing. You can just sit and be static. You can live the same life today that you lived yesterday. You will not change, but the world will change around you. You will sit still while everything else moves forward. Doing nothing is moving backward. It is getting stupider. The world is bigger, faster, richer, smarter, and more interesting every day. If you want to participate in all of this exciting change, you need to take steps to be part of it.

Many people fear that keeping up with the world is just too hard. But the world is a big place and it moves very slowly. Most people are able to keep up with the world and pass through life with just a small amount of effort. Moving the world forward is like moving an army of thousands down a road. To stay together, a thousand people and vehicles have to move relatively slowly. Have you ever gotten behind a caravan of military vehicles on the highway? They are driving at 40 mph when the speed limit is 65 mph. It is not because those green trucks cannot move any faster. It is because if they go faster, they cannot stay together. Some vehicles will get lost. Some will speed ahead. Some will fall behind. In just an hour, they would be separated by miles. That is how the world moves forward. And like the traffic around the military convoy, you can move faster than this.

People fall behind and get stupider because they decide to park on the side of the road. They just give up and stop moving altogether. If you reject the ideas in this book, you are probably pulling over to the side of the road. You are probably planning on sitting still while the world moves past you.

Getting stupider is easy. But it is boring, painful, and punishing in the long term.

Get back on the road. Create a map, set your milestones, and start celebrating your journey through life.

Lazy—Not Today

A reporter from the local newspaper is touring a large factory on the edge of town. The factory is the largest employer in the area and the reporter is very interested in knowing how many people work in the facility. After visiting the factory floor and talking with a number of managers, the reporter, while sitting with the general manager of the facility, asks, *"How many people work here?"*

The general manager thinks for a moment and replies, *"About half of them."*

That is an old joke. It is still funny because of its surprising honesty. Most people do not work anywhere. They might have a job. They might be paid every month. They might be part of the rat race to "get to work" every morning. But the one thing they avoid doing once they are at work is "work." Have you ever visited a fast food restaurant at a time when the crew seemed to be moving particularly slowly? They did not have the usual hustle and bustle that you saw in the past. You notice that several people were standing around chatting with each other instead of helping customers. You notice that several empty tables still had food wrappers on them. What is one of the first things that you say to yourself when this happened? You may think, *"There is clearly not a manager on duty right now."* Without direct supervision, many people just shift into low gear. Some slip all the way into park. But when the manager walks in, suddenly work restarts again.

How many people actually work there? About half of them.

7 Deadly Sins

The idea of "seven deadly sins" started in the Proverbs of King Solomon. But the modern concept of a list of seven mortal, cardinal, or deadly sins was introduced by a fourth century monk named Evagrius Ponticus. It was adopted and modified by Pope Gregory I in 590AD. He promoted the seven deadly sins as:

1. Extravagance;
2. Gluttony;
3. Avarice or greed;
4. Acedia or discouragement;
5. Wrath;
6. Envy; and
7. Pride.

A later modernization of this list changed "extravagance" to "lust" and "discouragement" to "sloth." Sloth is also known as laziness.

Organized religion is an expression of the mores of society. It expresses what society believes about the world and about people. The 7 Deadly Sins make it clear that laziness is one of the worst offenses that you can commit against your fellow citizen. Why is that? Laziness seems so passive—so "not evil." Laziness is not like murder, where you really hurt

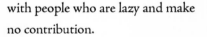

someone. Laziness is just like resting a little before you really get into your job.

Solomon also stated that, *"laziness leads to poverty."*—Proverbs 6:9–11

That seems a little harsh. Perhaps laziness is just the transition from resting to working. Perhaps it is just a natural part of the cycle between rest and work. Why would social and religious leaders consider laziness to be so bad?

Experience
We have learned how dangerous and destructive laziness can be through thousands of years of experience with people dedicated to their work and to making a contribution to society, and through thousands of years of the same experience

with people who are lazy and make no contribution.

In any society struggling to feed itself, to produce clothing, to keep its people healthy, the laziness of a few members can threaten the survival or health of many more. Society is a large, interconnected machine. The actions of each person affect many others around them. Laziness eliminates some productivity from the community. It takes away a small part of everyone's wealth.

Imagine that you live in a small village with a single baker who provides bread. If the baker is industrious and hard working, he may produce enough bread so that everyone in the village can eat as much as they can afford to purchase. He makes a good living for himself. He also insures that people are getting enough food to be healthy and to have the energy they need to do their own work.

Now imagine another village down the road. In this village, the baker is very lazy. He had the skills and tools to produce just as much bread as his brother in the first village. But he chooses not to do so. Instead, he spends much more time sleeping, drinking, and just wandering the streets. His actions have a direct impact on the entire village. They still have enough bread to survive. But they are slightly undernourished. They have a little less energy than if they were better fed. The entire village is affected by the behavior of this one man. The entire village is less healthy. The entire village produces fewer goods of all kinds because they are tired and undernourished. This entire village will be poorer and less able to compete with the output of the other villages around them, all because of the laziness of a single but essential person in the village.

Laziness does not just have personal consequences. It has a trickledown effect on dozens or hundreds of other people. It can hold back an entire community and even an entire nation. Communist Russia was founded on the ideal that each person would receive an equal share of the wealth of society, regardless of how much they individually contributed. This created an incentive for people to be lazy because working harder did not lead to more food, better housing, better clothing, or more security. In Russia, both laziness and hard work produced the same result, so most people opted for laziness. Since huge numbers of people did this, the entire country became poorer and missed out on the huge growth in wealth, health, and technical progress from World War II through the 1990s, and they are still feeling the effects today.

Nature of Mind and Body

As a human being, you are blessed with a very powerful mind and body. Both of these are designed to be active. Your body is a machine made to move you around and to interact with the world you are in. The machine is based on a collection of bones, muscles, and nerves that can perform amazing feats of strength, dexterity, and creativity. When you step on a scale, on average between 36% and 42% of your weight is muscle. More than one-third of all of your body is designed to move you around—to make you active. An additional 14% of your body mass is made up of bones. This is the framework that allows your muscles to carry your entire body from place to place, or to perform physical maneuvers. Your body atrophies when it is not active. It grows weaker. It is more prone to disease. The human body is made to be active.

The human mind is also designed for activity. It is tied to all five major senses and sends commands throughout the body. It is constantly working on inputs from the eyes, ears, nose, mouth, and skin. It carries on a constant internal conversation about all of the information it has received in the past and during the present. It is never idle.

You are a machine made for physical and mental action. Action is a natural human behavior. Laziness is completely counter to the nature of the kind of animal that you are. Despite this, many people feel that their mind and body are telling them to be inactive. They believe that they are programmed to be lazy. They do not believe that action is the core purpose of their mind and body. Why is that? This belief comes from misprogramming and misaligning both the body and the mind. Shifting from lazy to active will require realigning your body and mind.

Moving From Lazy To Active

Becoming active is not just throwing the "on" switch. Parents often try to motivate their children to action with statements like:

> *"Why don't you just get up and do something?"*
> *"Are you going to sit there all day?"*
> *"Stop being so lazy?"*

These are the results they are looking for, but they do not tell their children how to "want" to be active rather than "wanting" to be lazy. Somehow, children need to find the energy to shift from being lazy to being active. Where will that energy come from?

Energy from Food

The first and most obvious source of energy is food. You have to make sure that your body is healthy and well fueled to be active. In the same way that caffeine gives you a jolt of energy to get moving, other healthy habits can change the way you feel and think about being active. New healthy habits can give you twice as much energy as you have right now.

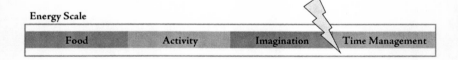

Energy Scale

| Food | Activity | Imagination | Time Management |

We want to start by getting some good fuel into your body. Your body needs a few basic foods to create the energy that you are looking for and to get stronger. Each day, you need to give your body a dose of the following:

1. **Fruit.** Two pieces of raw fruit every day. You can choose any two you like. Have one at breakfast and the second with lunch. Since fruits are very compact and portable, you can store them at home and carry them to work even if you are eating out.

2. **Vegetables.** One vegetable each day, preferably raw. A salad at lunch is a great way to do this. Or, have a carrot with your lunch or celery with dinner.

3. **Milk.** Drink a glass of milk every morning with breakfast or every evening before dinner. You just need one glass to increase your energy level.

4. **Grains.** Include whole grain bread or cereal in one of your meals.

5. **Protein.** The American diet consists almost completely of carbohydrates and fat. Protein is more expensive and therefore snack foods exclude this as an ingredient. You need two good servings of protein every day. This may be a piece of meat, chicken, turkey, fish, tofu, cheese, or milk. At lunch or dinner, have a turkey or chicken sandwich on whole grain bread. At breakfast, start making yourself protein drinks.

6. **Vitamin Supplement.** Your body is a machine that is much more complicated than an automobile or a computer. It is a flesh bag full of chemical and electrical reactions that depend on the presence of hundreds of ingredients to function well. In America, we have little problem getting all of the calories we need to survive. But we do a poor job of getting the nutrients that make the body function at its peak. Pick any multivitamin on the market and take one every day.

7. **Sunlight.** Exposure to the UV radiation in sunlight assists your body in creating vitamin D. It also warms the tissues causing increased blood flow. The bright-

ness of the world and the radiation absorbed improves your mood and your thoughts about life.

These seven simple changes to your eating habits will make a huge difference in how you feel about being active. They can easily double the amount of energy you have and increase your willingness to use that energy.

These seven changes are not a complete prescription for healthy living. You can learn about and do a lot more if you choose to. These are simply the basic and easy steps that you can take to get the energy you need to be more active.

Energy from Activity

Your body is a machine for action. You need to put it through its paces every day. Take some time every day and get active. Exercise can be like a crossword puzzle for your body. It takes only a few minutes, but it makes a big difference in how sharp and fit you are.

This is a book about overcoming the four major failures of life. It is not an exercise and diet book. But you cannot change the way you think and behave without improving the fitness of both your body and your mind. A basic exercise routine that helps you build the energy to escape your laziness will take 30 minutes every day. The goal of this routine is to circulate the blood, strengthen the muscles, and create heavy breathing. You can accomplish this with any form of activity that turns you on.

Start by trying every activity that you think you are interested in. Keep trying them until you find the one, two, or three that you can stick with every day for a year or more. These activities can be as easy as walking around the block. Lift weights in front of the television. Bicycling. Running. Swimming. Playing tennis. Calisthenics. Stretching. We have invented so many different types of physical exercise and sports that there is something that you will like.

Put your body to work for 30 minutes every day.

Energy from Imagination

The next energy creator that we recommend is visualization. Visualization is also called affirmation. Take five minutes a day to imagine achieving the goals you are pursuing. You can imagine by meditating with your eyes closed. You can imagine by describing your goals to yourself in the mirror. You can imagine by looking at pictures. You can imagine by acting out what will happen. You can imagine by writing your goals in words.

The goal is for you to see the positive outcome of all of your work. Many people only think about the negative things that have happened in their lives or that they fear are coming in the future. You can choose to think about just as many positive things. Everyone's past has some great memories that can occupy the mind. Everyone's future has wonderful potential that you can spend your time imagining.

Your mind is programmable. You have been programming it for your entire life. If you do not like how it thinks, you need to start changing the way you program it. You need to start thinking about the things that excite you, encourage you, and motivate you to take action.

Stop thinking about the terrible past and the scary future. Think about the wonderful past and the exciting future. If you have been negatively programming your mind for years, then you have learned to associate bad thoughts with many of the people, places, and things that you see every day. Changing this reaction may take a little help. One form of help that you can use is a talisman.

A talisman was originally an amulet or a small object engraved with magical symbols that could ward off evil. However, the magic behind these objects has always been in the mental associations attached to them. Talismans ward off evil by focusing the owner's mind on good things, by redirecting their actions toward good choices and away from evil choices. They do not have any special power, except what they trigger in the human mind.

If you live in a world that only reminds you of negative and bad ideas, then you may use a talisman associated with your new positive and active images. This talisman will remind you to think about and to take actions that are positive and constructive.

Christianity has always used talismans to remind people to act and think according to Biblical principles. The small cross necklaces that many people wear are more than jewelry. They are reminders to the wearers that they are trying to be like God. People who wear these will often rub or hold them when they are trying to remember to behave in a godly manner. The power is not in the metal of the necklace, but in the mental associations that they have with this object and its shape.

As you exchange lazy for active, stupid for smart, ugly for attractive, and afraid for bold, you may find a talisman to be very helpful in reminding you to think and act in a different way. There are a number of good ideas for these kinds of talismans. We will describe these in a later chapter.

Change the way you think to change the way you behave.

Energy from Time Management

You will also find yourself more able to take action to deal with the world if you are in control of your time. Many people are lazy and tired because they have lost control of the time necessary to master their lives. They have turned their daily and weekly schedules over to bad habits that waste and squander the time that makes up their life.

When you cannot control your time, giving up on the activities that can help you be more alive and more successful is almost natural. Without the time to do these activities, the thought of attempting them is just tiring and defeating.

Conversely, when you control your time, you will find that you are able to be active in changing your life. You will find that you can break up big goals and work on them in reasonable, manageable, and realistic pieces. Once you control your time you can accomplish very, very large goals by taking them one small daily step at a time.

How can you gain control of your time? How can you turn the tables on your old habits of wasting time or letting other people control it?

1. Wake Up Earlier.

The first step is simply to get out of bed. You need to get out of bed at a time that allows you to meet your goals. Not at a time when your mind and body feel like waking up. How much sleep does a person need? We often talk of eight hours as a common average. So begin with that number. You get out of bed eight hours after you go to bed. Not nine hours and not eight and a half. Cut your sleeping back to eight hours. As you keep this up, it will become a habit and your body will adjust to eight hours as being a normal amount of sleep. In fact, as you become a more active person, you will find that your mind and body begin to sleep fewer hours. You might settle at seven hours. Some people live their entire lives on four or five hours of sleep a night because that is what their mind and body have adjusted to.

2. Get Moving Faster.

Getting out of bed is the first step—but not the only step.
Next, you need to get moving sooner. Finish your morning
routine of cleaning, dressing, and eating in one hour or less.
You should be ready to begin your day one hour after you
wake up. Taken together, these first two steps give you back
one, two, or three hours in your day. For some people, even
more.

3. Go to Bed Earlier.

If you stick to sleeping eight hours a day, you will get tired
and sleepy at the same time each night. The end of your day
will become more regular and you will have to stop wasting
away hours with passive activities like watching television or
drinking socially.

4. Do What is Important.

Given all of the things you can be doing with your life and
your newly acquired time, which should you choose to do?

You need to prioritize all of the things you could do, all of
the things you want to do, and all of the things that can help
you reach your goals.

Every day, when you think about what you could do today,
single out the one or two things that are most important.
Move these to the top of the list. Make sure that you spend
time on each of these every day. Do not let your important

activities get pushed aside and relegated to the weekend or a few minutes before you go to bed. Do the important things when you are the most alert and sharp.

5. Set Goals

If you do not have any goals for your life or your day, then there really is little reason to get up in the morning. There is little reason to "get moving faster" because you do not have anything worth doing or anyplace worth going. Goals are the motivation of life. We all have small goals. These are the motivations that carry us to the refrigerator because we are hungry. These are the urges that advertisers generate to get us to see a movie. These motivations create small goals that come and go every day . But you will notice that these are repetitive. They accomplish one very small thing. Then they subside, and return the next day or the next week. These goals never accumulate into anything significant. These goals are the same as the goals that motivate animals. Your dog or cat is motivated continuously and repetitively by these types of goals.

You need goals that are larger, that last longer, and are more exciting than just sleep-eat-work-play ... repeat.

Entire books have been written on goal setting. Goal setting is a process of writing down a list of the things that your mind and your heart really want to accomplish on this earth. These are the things that you feel you were put here to con-

tribute to. Accomplishing these is how your life will make
a difference in the world. Your goals may be small from a
global perspective but you are looking for things that are important and essential to you.

Everyone has different goals. That is why such diversity exists in the world. Some people are driven to care for the hungry in their neighborhood or city. Others are called to care
for the spiritual needs of their neighbors. Some people are
compelled to create new movies or buildings for the world
to enjoy. Some must write books. Some breed dogs. But everything you see around you exists and is happening because
someone had a goal or a calling to contribute to the world.

What is your goal? What is your calling? Why are you here?
What will you contribute?

The answer to these questions makes up your own list of
goals.

These goals will motivate you. They will give you a reason to
get out of bed, a reason to start early, a reason to take control
of your time, a reason to prioritize the ways that you can
spend your time and energy.

6. Will It.
Goals and physical energy are not always sufficient to make
you active. Despite these, there are times when your mind

will work against you. Your mind and your inner fears can conspire to stop you dead in your tracks. There are times when you are just not motivated to work toward your goals. There are times when you will feel paralyzed in bed or in a soft chair. You know what you **wish** you wanted to do right now. But you believe that you just cannot get up and do it. Your mind will paralyze you.

At these times, you need to resort to brute force—brute mental force. You need to will yourself to do it. You need to will yourself right out of the chair and into action. Your internal will needs to take over and give commands to your body and your mind to get going.

Some people have developed a will strong enough to overcome all physical and mental resistance. You read about the gymnast who gets up every morning at 4 am so she can begin training by 5 am. You read about stock traders who rise early enough to catch the opening of the stock market in another country. These people have chosen a life that requires them to exercise their will every day.

Most of us have not had this kind of practice or have not exercised our will in this way. Most of us have a weak, flabby will than has not been exercised in weeks or years. But, just like your body, regular practice will build up the strength of your will. It will develop "will muscle tone." You can become a bodybuilder of your own will—a will-builder.

Start ordering your body and your mind to do what you want them to do and you will find your will-muscles growing every day.

7. Schedule.

Write down a schedule for your day and your week. Use a calendar that shows the hours of each day. Block off the times that you will sleep, eat, and work. Between these times, schedule the activities that you want to accomplish for the week. Put them into their places and use this schedule to help you get them done.

A written schedule like this is a great tool to help you build your will. You can see when something needs to get done and you can see why it would be bad to slip on that job. You can see that the day, the week, and the year are not limitless. You really do run out of time for getting things done. The future becomes much less misty and uncertain when you have a schedule to help you look into the future.

You will notice that your job takes up a big block of time right in the middle of your day. This block should also contain scheduled items. Whatever your job, you should be able to schedule specific tasks during the day to help you do it better. You can schedule the time that you work in the same way that you schedule your free time. Both contribute to your future. Both carry you forward toward some destination. They are either carrying you to a destination that you have chosen, or they carry you toward a destination that is chosen for you by someone else. A schedule is one way for you to take control of the boat and steer it toward your own goals and your own destinations.

8. Milestones.

The Romans conquered huge pieces of Europe. One of the major tools they used to rule this large area was the first highway system in the world. They built a series of roads that allowed their politicians, tax collectors, and armies to travel quickly to every part of their empire.

Along these roads they placed markers that gave the traveler an indication of their location. These might have written on them the distance from Rome or from a nearby landmark like a city, mountain, or river. These milestones allowed travelers to see their progress toward their destination and to make plans to adjust their travel. Without these milestones, it was unclear how far a traveler had gone and how far ahead their destination lay.

You need to place similar milestones in your life. You have a destination or a goal to achieve. But you should also have milestones that tell you how well you are progressing toward your goals. A milestone marks a significant event or accomplishment. It can also mark a specific amount of effort or days devoted to a goal.

When you write a book, the completion of a chapter is a milestone toward a larger goal.

When you climb a mountain, specific points mark the conquering of a difficult ridge or face.

When you are selling cars, boats, or houses, there will be points at which you will have made significant progress toward your overall goal.

Milestones show you and the world that you are making progress. They convince your mind that you will accomplish the goal because you have already come so far.

Milestones are also an opportunity for celebration. They indicate a point at which you need to congratulate and reward yourself for your good work. They indicate a point of refreshment and encouragement. In fact, the enjoyment of one milestone can create the motivation to get you moving toward the next one.

All of life is a journey, not a destination. Milestones allow you to stop and enjoy the progress that you are making in your journey. For most of us, every big goal is actually a milestone in a much larger plan for our lives.

When you create your goals and set a schedule for attaining them, you must also identify milestones along the way.

These mark significant points of accomplishment and mark a time for celebration.

Tricks of the Action Trade

In addition to all of the above advice on turning your laziness into action, active people use a number of tricks to keep themselves going. Each person learns these over the years and begins practicing them to be more active than their mind might otherwise let them be.

1. Action Trigger

When your mind and body say they are not ready to get started, there is often a little action that you can take to change that attitude. This action is not necessarily your main objective, but it is something that will change your mind in a positive way.

For example, on weekends I like to start my days with a short two-mile run from my house. But on the weekends, my body usually does not feel like jumping into running clothes as soon as I get out of bed. I have learned that if I just step out the back door and smell the fresh morning air, it will change everything. A whiff of that air and a look at the morning sky usually wake me up and make me want to be out there. Rather than brute force willing myself to go running, I start by stepping out for the breath of fresh air that will trigger my desired run.

There are triggers like this for most of your activities as well. You just have to notice them.

When I do not feel like writing, I convince myself to sit down and read the last page that I previously wrote. This is often enough to get the juices flowing and to get my mind to thinking about what I want to write next. I don't force myself to write; rather, I force myself to read, which triggers the desire to write.

2. Short List

Goals, schedules, and lists of things to do are very helpful. But psychologists have found that people are often paralyzed by long lists of things to do. If your mind is faced with far too many things to organize, you can become confused and just stop taking action.

The best way to overcome this is to replace the long list with a very short list. Make a short list of just three things that you want to get done in the next hour or the next day. That list is very manageable and something that you can take action on right now. Once those three items are done, you can create a new shirt list. Don't think about the long list, just focus on the short list of three.

3. Play

You cannot work all of the time and you cannot take work as a completely serious activity. You have to play. You have to release and entertain the inner child that insists that life is fun. You can take a break from work to play, to have fun, to do something silly and light. You need to take these kinds of breaks as a form of renewal. They do not have to be long, but they do have to be something that you really enjoy. Allow yourself to turn your back on work for a few minutes or a few hours.

You can also play while at work. Many people have a job in which it is OK to turn on the fun factor while working. You can kid around with your coworkers, have a competition, or just go crazy for a few minutes. If you can do this on your job, then take advantage of it and incorporate play into your workday.

This play-on-the-job behavior does not fit into every job. People who work in the medical field, law enforcement, and in legal positions need to be very careful not to display this type of behavior to customers and clients. They should also avoid playing in an unprofessional manner.

4. *Tell Someone*

When you describe what you are doing to another person, you first have to build a clear picture and a set of words in your own mind. When you do this, it become clearer to you exactly how you will be getting something done. You will see around some of the fears and obstacles that were haunting you. Fuzzy ideas about how to do something can more easily conceal fears. When you sharpen the ideas by describing them to others, the fear will disappear with the fuzziness. The act of telling someone else makes the action more real in your own mind. When you talk about the action, it engages a different part of your brain and makes you smarter in dealing with the problem.

Telling other people about it also creates an internal obligation. You feel bound to accomplish your goals because other people know about them, will ask about them in the future, and will know if you give up.

5. Have a Partner

Better than just telling another person is asking someone to join you. Get a partner. Butch Cassidy had the Sundance Kid. Clyde had Bonnie. Lewis had Clark. Laurel had Hardy. Abbott had Costello. The President has the Vice President. You do not need to tackle everything by yourself. Plenty of people in the world are pursuing similar goals. When you find one of them, ask him or her to work with you.

One of the most powerful ingredients in the Weight Watchers program is getting people to work together. Two or three people with the same goals can support and encourage each other. They can also share ideas on how to get there, making the team two or three times smarter.

6. Multitasking

Multitasking means having two, or three, or four things going at the same time. If you have three goals that you are working toward, then you have choices on what you are going to do right now. As you work toward one goal, you might become tired or lose your enthusiasm for it after an hour or two. This is the time to switch to one of your other goals. It provides a fresh set of activities, a new mindset, different tools, and different information. Instead of stopping work toward a goal because you are fatigued, you can switch to working on a different goal.

By ping-ponging back and forth, you can make progress on three different things during an afternoon before you get too tired to continue working. This is better than working on one thing for an hour, losing your mental focus, then quitting for the day.

Beware of trying to run more than three or four of these activities simultaneously. If you try to do too many activities, you will run into a mental gridlock of confusion. You will not be able to work on any of them because you are trying to juggle too many in your head at the same time.

These are just a few of the tricks that effective people use to get more done that most of the people around them.

Wrapping It Up

We have talked about a number of strategies that you can use to switch from being lazy to being active. Start by changing the fuel that you put into your body. Give yourself the food and the vitamins that your body needs to generate energy. Then exercise your body in some way so that it is fit enough to carry you into activity. Visualize what you will accomplish. Use verbal affirmations to explain your goals and actions to yourself. Finally, be in control of your own time. Create more time and more organization throughout your day so that you have the time you need to work toward your goals.

If you are a chronically lazy person, this will be a slow process. But it is simply a process of retraining your mind and body to behave differently than you have trained them to behave in the past. Just keep going and you will see daily progress.

CHAPTER

8

Ugly—Remade

When you are ugly, you set yourself against the rest of the world. You put yourself in a position where you have repelled everyone else around you and you have to face and solve every problem by yourself. You do not have a relationship with others that will cause them to empathize with you and contribute to solving the problems that you find important.

This can be as simple as getting your spouse's help working on the garden, or as significant as getting help finding a new job. Both of these jobs benefit greatly from the assistance of other people. In fact, almost everything you are trying to do in life can benefit from the assistance of other people.

Shifting from ugly to attractive is not something you do just to make other people in the world happy; it also directly impacts every part of your internal life. When you are ugly, the people around you attempt to isolate, control, and destroy you. Their goal is to eliminate your ugliness from their life experience. As a result, being ugly is extremely detrimental to your life goals and aspirations. It is almost impossible to succeed when everyone around you is seeking to destroy you.

In 1624, John Donne wrote the famous words, *"no man is an island, entire of itself."* He observed that though an island may be completely separated from larger bodies of land, men are not like that. We are all part of a larger body. We all contribute to that larger body and are benefited by being part of it.

Ugliness is an attempt by man to separate from the body of mankind and live as an island—small, inconsequential, unproductive, and lonely. Ugliness makes you a poor and empty island.

The passage by Donne on this subject is actually quite a bit longer than that single phrase. Read the entire paragraph.

> *"All mankind is of one author, and is one volume; when one man dies, one chapter is not torn out of the book, but translated into a better language; and every chapter must be so translated...As therefore the bell that rings to a sermon, calls not upon the preacher only, but upon the congregation to come: so this bell calls us all: but how much more me, who am brought so near the door by this sickness....No man is an island, entire of itself... any man's death diminishes me, because I am involved in mankind; and therefore never send to know for whom the bell tolls; it tolls for thee."*
> **John Donne, Meditation XVII, 1624**

In the natural world, cheetahs are successful because they can run faster than their prey. Tigers and lions are stealthy and strong enough to bring down large antelope. Snakes are equipped with venom and fangs. Rabbits are able to run quickly through underbrush and reproduce in large numbers. But what about man? Why is man so successful? It is not because of our large muscles, fangs, speed, or stealth. Man is successful because of his intelligence and his social ability. Humans have built large societies, buildings, roads, schools, computers, rockets, radios, and thousands of amazing inventions. All of these rely on our intelligence and our ability to work together. None of the great accomplishments were done by a single human. They have all come from cooperation among a few, a hundred, or a thousand people.

When you choose to be ugly to those around you, you are cutting yourself off from one of the most powerful forces that humans have used to be successful in the natural and social world.

You cannot succeed without help from other people.

You cannot reach your goals alone and unaided.

You cannot even survive alone.

Being attractive in personality and developing connections with other people is an essential survival trait. It is also essential for you to reach your goals and to leave a lasting contribution in the world.

Exchanging Ugly for Attractive

You cannot exchange ugly behaviors for attractive ones
unless you are able to identify those that are holding you
back—and the alternatives that you can use to replace them.
Taking an introspective look at ourselves is a difficult thing
to do. It requires that we look past the blame that we connect to the outside world and to think about our own faults,
our own responsibilities. Recognize these calls for us to accept blame and to accept the job of repairing the damage we
have done to ourselves and others.

Your first reaction to this introspection might be to place the
blame for your ugliness on other people. You might quickly
point the finger to external forces and people, and claim that
you cannot change until those externals change. This is the
prisoner mentality. This is the inner view that you are a prisoner of other people. They are the prison warden, guard, cell
boss. You are just doing what they order you to do and have
no control and no authority over your own life.

This is a false view for every free person in society. It is also a
false view for every prisoner in captivity.

One Page Life Story
Throughout history, prisoners of war have discovered that
they do indeed possess a great deal of power over their own
minds and behavior despite being a physical prisoner. A

number of accounts of physical and psychological survival of prisoners exists from WWII, the Korean War, and the Vietnam War.

In all of these stories, the survivors recognized the essential importance of separating their external physical condition from their internal mental condition. Though they were locked up, starving, freezing, or being tortured, there remained an inner life—an inner light. This light could not be doused by external treatment, but remained alive and strong. It retained the joy of memories past and the hope of seeing loved ones again.

Your first exercise is to write your own life story on a single piece of paper. I want you to write a summary of how you came to be who you are right now. It can be quick and to the point. Capture the people, places, and situations that have brought you to your current place in life.

One page is enough for many people. But others find this exercise so engrossing that they go on for two, three, and even more pages. The words just flow out of them like they have been waiting for someone to ask this question for years. Like a broken dam, the pent up emotions and stories come rushing out.

Once this story is written, I want you to move to a new seat in the house. I want you to take on a different perspective. I want you to read it as if you were a different person. You are going to look at this story from the eyes of others to see and hear what others see and hear in your story.

Does this story describe a victim of situations and other people? Did this person have a say over who he or she has became or did the person give the outside world complete control? Or, was this person in control of his or her life and development? Is he or she the hero of the story? Does he or she determine how to react and where to go?

Is this the story of a victim of life or a hero of life?

Trait Transplant

As you identify the ugliness that you will change into attractiveness, you must separate the external connections to that ugliness from the internal response that you generate to it. Your internal response will be different. You cannot change everything that you do not like about the outside world. But you can change the way your internal world reacts to it.

As you identify your ugly trait, you must also identify an attractive alternative trait. You will give yourself a trait transplant. You cannot remove the old trait and leave the space empty. You must replace it with a more attractive, valuable, and powerful attractive trait.

Take another sheet of paper and label it the "Trait Transplant." You will use this to find ways to replace your ugly traits with something more attractive, positive, and constructive. In most cases, your ugly trait is triggered by a specific situation. This situation triggers your ugly response, and it will trigger your mental decision to respond differently.

Describe a situation that brings out your ugly trait. Follow that situation with a description of the ugly trait itself and how other people see and feel about that trait coming from you. Then describe the attractive trait that you want to replace with the ugly trait.

Trait Transplant

Situation:	
Ugly Trait:	Attractive Trait:

The following table shows one example of this.

Situation:	
When my boss criticizes my work and points out additional information that I was not aware of, I begin to babble more details in an attempt to justify my own position and actions. I am trying to make him understand my perspective and see that I made a good choice give the information I had at the time.	
Ugly Trait: *This shows insecurity and an unwillingness to learn. What your boss sees is your justification. He cannot determine whether you listened to his input or what you are going to do with it.*	Attractive Trait: *When your boss provides additional information, answer with something like, "I see. I did not know that." When he corrects your actions, reply with, "I understand and I will get right on it." Make sure that he knows that you have heard him and that you respect his advice. After he knows that you have heard him, you may be able to add details. Do not use detail-babbling to try to preserve your own ego. Accept correction, assistance, and criticism.*

In most cases, your ugly behavior does not come from some mysterious cave of feelings that you cannot look into. It comes from the ongoing inner dialog that you have with yourself about your life. Your mind is running a constant movie about the past and the future. It shows scenes from what has happened and what you fear will happen. These movies about the future usually reflect fear more often than hope. We learn to anticipate the negative things that will happen and run mental movies about those that we want reinforce over and over.

More successful and attractive people have learned to create a different kind of movie. In their minds, they are watching a movie about the positive hope that they have for the future. They have created movies that show good outcomes of future situations and actions. They are reinforcing and preparing their minds for attractive behavior in response to future events.

This movie selection is a choice that we all make. The movies themselves are not real and they are not accurate. But they are training and preparation ground for how we will react in the future. You can choose to watch attractive movies or ugly movies about yourself. Neither is accurate about the future but both are a statement about what we plan to do when the future does happen. Creating positive movies is not a lie. Creating negative movies is not a noble truth. Each is a choice. Each will determine how you react when the future does happen.

Choose to make and watch positive movies that show yourself with attractive traits.

Angry

Many people find it difficult or impossible to exchange their ugly behavior for attractive behavior because they are angry. They hold deep anger against some people around them right now or against others from the past that had a significant negative impact on them. This may be a parent, spouse, sibling, neighbor, former lover, coworker, boss, or even a stranger. That relationship acts as a poison in their system every day. They are reminded once, twice, three times, or even dozens of times a day of the person and their reasons for being angry. This deep residing anger stands as a barrier to eliminating ugly traits. In many cases, the anger is the source of the ugly trait. Abandoning the ugliness means releasing the anger and requires forgetting or forgiving the person believed to be the source of this anger.

The anger has become habitual. It is a daily part of who you are. Without meaning to, you have ingested, digested, and incorporated anger and a piece of your worst enemy into your own body and mind. Over the years, this person or a specific event has become as much a part of you as your arm or leg. You cannot imagine being without that anger and that memory any more than you can imagine being without an arm or leg.

No one intends to ingest such poisonous memories of their past. Most people do not realize that remembering the problem over and over is driving it deeper and deeper into their mind. They just believe that it is a passing emotion. They expect to be angry for a day or two and then think that the anger will go away. But, years later they notice that any thought of the person or situation makes them furious. They notice that when a similar person or situation comes into their life, they immediately react with a negative internal emotion and a very ugly exterior response. They assume that this residual comes from the outside and is just something that will return from time to time. However, exactly the opposite happens. The anger is internal. It is burrowed deep into their psyche and lays dormant. It is inside them and continues to poison their thoughts, their actions, and their relationships for years, decades, or an entire lifetime.

If you want to change your ugliness into attractiveness, you will have to look directly at your internal anger, identify it, contain it, and excise it. Just as you would remove a splinter from your finger or a surgeon would remove cancer from your body, your anger cannot remain inside where it will poison you every day.

Look at this anger. Examine where it came from and why it is still with you. Get some idea for how it has affected your life in the months or years since you first ingested it. Acknowledge that you have it and that it is not a part of you.

Acknowledge that it is a foreign body that has gotten inside you and has grown attached to you.

Now contain the anger. When you recognize how it is connected to other events in your life, you can begin to sever those connections. Recognize that hundreds of people around you do not have this same poisonous anger inside them. The triggers that cause you to remember the angry past are not universal. They are unique to you. They are connections that only exist in your mind and body. These connections can be severed. These connections can be replaced with the same kind of healthy connections that hundreds of other people have. You must mentally separate what is happening to you right now from the event of your past that caused the anger. Then reconnect the current people and situations to good memories. Let your daily experiences remind you of good things, not bad.

Once separated from your life, you need to extract this anger. You need to convince yourself that the cause of your anger was something from the past that does not need to be part of your life forever. It has already lived inside of you for too long and it is time for that memory to die and leave your mind. You may never forget it. But you need to make it meaningless to you today. It is something that has no emotional attachments, no meaning, and no significance to what you are today.

This entire process can be carried out through prayer, meditation, visualization, verbal commands, or a combination of all of these tools. Prayer and meditation have been part of human culture since the beginning of man. They are tools that allow you to deal with your internal thoughts and feelings. Visualization and verbal affirmations are just as old. You can use all of them to exercise the anger and the demons that you have invited into your mind, and that have taken up long term residence there. It is not impossible to get rid of them. People have been doing it for centuries. In many cases, religious practice has been designed to provide the instructions, permission, and belief necessary to extract these. You can do the same.

When you can get the anger and the hurt out of your own mind, you will no longer find it necessary to hurt other people. You will not feel compelled to be ugly to people as a reflection of the ugliness inside of you. As you become attractive inside, you will reflect that attractiveness to the outside world. You will also come to believe that the outside world is deserving of attractive behavior and you will work to provide that.

Behave Attractively

After you have removed your anger and replaced ugly with attractive, you will find that you are not very comfortable in your new, attractive clothing. It will not feel natural to you. You will feel fake and out of place with all of the people who have known you as an ugly person. If you have been truly ugly, you have probably attracted a lot of friends who are similarly ugly. You will be used to a social life that revolves around exchanging ugly behavior with others. It will be difficult to be an attractive person while remaining part of this crowd.

You have changed but your old crowd has not. If you go back to them, then they will shift you back to your old ugliness. Part of your shift to attractiveness will involve attracting new people into your circle of daily acquaintances. Rest assured that you are not abandoning all of your old friends. Some of them are just as eager as you are to escape their ugliness and anger. You will see and feel them shift to a more attractive style. You will escape some of your acquaintances, but you will help a few of them make the break that they have been so eager for. So escaping your own failures will benefit you and some of those who are close to you. You will save someone from his or her own personal ugliness.

Even though your new behavior feels strange and foreign, you must keep it. Your attractive behaviors and traits are not wrong. They are just new and shaped differently. Your discomfort will pass as you learn to wear these new clothes more naturally and as you adapt them to your own personality and style.

Before you go out in public or engage someone in conversation, stop and adjust your new attractive self. Remind yourself of who you are now. Then go out and be attractive. Just keep doing it even if you find it tiring. It is like a new physical activity. You will use muscles and concentration that you are not familiar with yet. But you will develop a strength in attractiveness that is far beyond what you start with. Just keep acting attractive and you will continue to become more attractive.

If you become too tired trying to be attractive, then extract yourself from the crowd and the situation to rest, recharge, and recuperate. Then go at it again. When you reach the end of your attractive stamina, just go home, go to bed, and start again tomorrow.

Cleanup

Your outer appearance also reflects your personality traits. The ugliness that you feel and express can usually be seen in your style of dress, arrangement of office, and condition of home. As you become more personally attractive, you need to change your personal environment to match that new attractiveness. Changing this environment will also remove many reminders of your old traits and replace them with reminders of your new attractiveness.

The kinds of changes that we are talking about are currently the topic of many reality television programs. Normal people appear on these shows and allow experts to help them change their physical appearance, their style of dress, their behaviors, or the style of their home. You need to do a similar personal and home makeover so that your external world is a reflection and a reinforcement of your inner change.

On television there is always some kind of expert helping people to change. If you can recruit someone to help you, that is great. If you cannot, then you will have to be your own change expert by using the ideas in this book.

Body. First, look at your body. Is it clean and well kept? Are your finger and toenails trimmed and clean? Do you bathe daily? Is your skin supple and soft? If it has become weathered from outdoor work, look for a lotion that will help it look more like human skin and less like saddle leather.

Hair. Start with the hair on the top of your head. Do you cut it at least once a month? Is it washed every day? Do you have a style appropriate for this decade? The same goes for men's facial hair. Your beard or mustache should be a style that you have seen one other person wearing this week. You should also cut, clean, and groom it. It does not have to be short; it just has to be groomed and controlled, not running wild like a mountain man.

Clothing. Your clothing should be clean and have some shape to it. All of us have favorite items of clothing that we have worn until they are just like a sack that we throw over our heads. These are fine when you are mowing the grass or exercising. But these are not the kinds of clothing to wear in a public setting or around friends. You do not need to make an expensive shopping trip. Instead, it calls for putting everything through the washing machine and choosing to wear clothes that come out clean, odor free, and with some thickness still left.

Car. Many people treat their cars like a rolling trashcan. Empty all of the trash from the inside of your car. Clean the dash, carpets, and seats. If your car has a foul odor, clean out the source of the smell and install an air freshener inside. Wash the car and make it shine from the roof to the hubcaps.

Office. If you have your own office or cubicle area at work, it needs to be clean and professional. This is where you express to all of your coworkers and your bosses who you are and what they can expect from you. It cannot be filthy with food or wrappers. It should not be a disaster area of papers and working materials. Most functional offices have a few items that are "in process" on the desk or table. But the tops of the desk, table, and shelves are not stacked with remnants of projects from the past 20 years. Everyone has decorations in their office. These may be pictures of family, mementos, and clever artwork. Artists and creative types often surround themselves with toys that spur their imaginations. These are all good, as long as they are arranged to help you be creative and pro-ductive, and are not constantly in your way.

Home. Finally, there is your home. It needs to be clean and collected. An explosion of clutter is not "my style"; it is "your laziness" in not controlling the messes that you make. We live in our homes day-in and day-out. Your home is a functional place, not a show place. It is almost impossible to keep your home looking like the homes in magazine pictures, especially with more than one person living there. The goal is clean. We are not trying to be immaculate or psychotically perfect, just clean.

Giving all of these things, a makeover is difficult because we each see these places with different eyes. Working with a friend that you trust is a big help. They can make things more fun and help you see everything from someone else's perspective. We all have blind spots in our ability to see the world closest to us. But we also have friends who can help with this and who may be very eager to provide that help.

Mental Feng Shui

Feng Shui, pronounced *fung-shway*, is an ancient Chi-nese system of aesthetics believed to use the laws of both heaven and earth to improve life by receiving the positive energy from nature. This "qi" energy was first described in the *Book of the Burial* by Guo Pu sometime between 265 and 420 AD. The idea comes from the line:

"Qi rides the wind and scatters, but is retained when encountering water."
Guo Pu

When you bring wind and water together, you are in a place that can capture the qi energy.

Independent from the Chinese philosophy of aesthetics, we want to borrow the idea that you can take positive steps to influence and change the course of your life. Feng Shui is about personal control over your surroundings and the positive benefits that come from doing that correctly. We want to provide you with a few actions that you can take to help you grow from ugly to attractive. We want to put more energy into your life, not mystically, but through your own actions.

Monitor Your Thoughts

To keep your mind on the right track, keep track of your mind. Notice whether you are mentally criticizing and cutting other people down when they are talking. If you are, then learn to reverse that. When you see people, think of the good things that you know about them. Everyone has very good and positive traits that you can choose to notice, think about, and mention to them.

You may believe that you are able to think critical thoughts about people and keep them to yourself. You believe that you are able to separate your thinking from your words, body language, and facial expression. But you really can't do this. Your thoughts will prevent you from expressing positive acceptance or engagement with the people around you. This may be very blatant or very subtle. But it will show.

We have all met people who are just wonderful to be around. They seem to attract other people more that someone who speaks the very same words. They just "have a way with people." One thing that makes these people so attractive to others is that they think positive and attractive thoughts about the people around them and especially about those to whom they are talking. These positive thoughts emerge in the tone of their voice, their expressed emotion, body language, and facial expression. The message that all of these convey is much stronger than the words alone.

If you are going to become an attractive person in the world, you must think attractive thoughts about those around you.

Get the Facts

When building your mental opinion and feelings about people, do you have your facts straight? Are you sure that you understand them and their situation accurately? Most people do not bother with the facts. They make snap negative judgments about people and make little or no effort to really understand them. If you are going to connect with these people, you need to know more about them. You need to make the effort to hear their story. You need to know the facts before you criticize, praise, adore, or condemn them. You must be aware of whether your thoughts, opinions, and behaviors are based on facts that you have collected from reliable sources, or based on "facts" that you have created yourself.

Values

Ask whether your treatment of people is in line with your own values. Are you treating them in the manner that your value system dictates that people should be treated? Are you treating them according to the same value system that you expect people to apply to you?

This is the Golden Rule of Christianity. Do unto others as you would have them do unto you. This basic principle has been part of world society for at least 2000 years, perhaps much longer. It is one of the secrets of holding a society together. Violating this principle is the basis for many of our criminal punishments and for countries severing relationships with each other.

Use a consistent set of values for yourself and for others.

Rebuilding After the War

Your ugliness was created by a war. You have been at war with the world for many years. You have had victories and defeats. Some of those defeats have left you injured, maimed, angry, and vengeful. Your present is strongly influenced by that past. But your future does not have to be a mirror reflection of your past. You can let the past fade into the past. All of the powerful and positive lessons that you are learning in this book can become part of your present and can have a strong influence on the future that you choose to build for yourself.

Though you may have many battles in your past, you will not be defined by your defeats or your injuries. You will not inflict your anger and these defeats on all of the people you meet in the future. You will recover, rebuild, and rejoice in the future. You will become the attractive person that you have seen others be.

You will not remain the ugly person that you have learned to be in the past.

9

Afraid—Of Nothing

Fear is a basic emotion and survival trait of mankind. Fear keeps us from getting into fatal situations. We learn from watching others that certain situations can be dangerous or fatal. We also have tendency to be afraid of the unknown and anything that is new and unfamiliar to us. Fear stops us from doing things that can lead to great loss and death. But fear is not always rational or beneficial.

When we were a race living in caves, struggling against the elements to stay alive, and competing directly with the other animals for food, our internal fears could make the difference between life and death. Today, we live in a much safer and more secure environment. Very few direct threats to our survival exist. We can spend days walking outdoors and never encounter a single animal threatening to eat us. We can face every extreme form of weather and not be killed by the cold or the heat. In modern society, very few situations and animals have any real interest in harming us. But our fear instinct is still alive and active in our minds. It prevents us from pursuing opportunities that may not succeed, but that would be far from fatal. Today, fear does not separate life from death; rather, it separates us from opportunity.

Our fear reaction is too active. It is too careful. It is too protective. The media likes to use fear to get our attention. They paint a picture of the world, the city, and the neighborhood that is filled with all types of deadly threats. We are constantly told by news anchors, talk show hosts, and movie plots that lethal danger lurks around every corner. This is not true. The threats that actually exist are very small in number and isolated in location, and generally do not exist in our neighborhoods, social circles, or professional environments. These voices make you more afraid than you should be. They cause you to hide from opportunities and limit your life to a very small, constricting area.

Fear stops you from being a modern human. It tries to move you backward to a state more like that of the caveman, who was afraid of animals, nature, and the unknown. In the twenty-first century, we face little threat to our lives. The bar of survival has moved much higher. The unknown and untested can damage the fringes of your life, but not the strong core of your physical and social survival.

It is time to be bold. It is time to put the caveman behind you and embrace the opportunities of the rich modern world all around you.

Becoming Bold

How do you become bold? What can you do to overcome both the innate fear instinct and your own personally constructed wall of fear? Both can be controlled and overcome. Millions of people just like you have learned to control their fear and take action despite the nagging voice of fear.

Mark Twain recognized the fear in his own life. He understood that he could never banish it completely, but had to learn to act despite the fear. A famous quote that he contributed to literature and to the psyche of the American personality is:

"Courage is resistance to fear, mastery of fear—not absence of fear."
Mark Twain

He understood that he could never completely banish, silence, and remove the fear in his own life. But he did have the power to resist the fear and to take action despite it. The following steps will help you do the same in your life.

Assess Your World

Examine your world. Look at the life you are living. Look at the things you want to do with your life but that fear is preventing you from tackling. How many risky ventures or projects do you have going? Do you have any? Are you striving to accomplish something new, something more? Or are you settled into a comfortable pattern that allows little or no change—little or no growth—little or no challenges—little or no excitement?

If you still have dreams and goals of doing more, then you need to overcome and master you fear before those dreams and goals die.

Assess the life you want to live. Ask yourself what is really threatening about the things you are afraid to try. What can really happen if you fail at them? Make a list of the goals you want to try to achieve and the very worst thing that can happen if you try but fail to achieve it. This is important because most of us create monsters in our minds that are much larger and more terrible than what can really happen in real life. Be real. Be honest. Force that monster out of the closet and into the light. Look at it from every direction and really understand the worst thing that can happen.

Now, realize that the worst thing is not the most likely thing. The worst is rare. Something much less severe and terrifying is more likely, more common, and more bearable.

In response to a reader who asked her about the fears of life ahead, Ann Landers provided a very settling piece of advice. She said to this person:

> *"If I were asked to give what I considered the single most useful bit of advice for all humanity, it would be this: Expect trouble as an inevitable part of life, and when it comes, hold your head high. Look it squarely in the eye and say, 'I will be bigger than you. You cannot defeat me.'"*
> **Ann Landers**

We have to understand that problems and troubles will happen in our lives. Some will come as a surprise and we will cause others ourselves. In both cases, we have to decide ahead of time that we will be bigger, stronger, and more resilient than our problems. We can decide ahead of time that we will not be defeated by our problems. We can decide ahead of time that we will be stronger and more persistent than any problem.

If you are young and inexperienced and have problems, these words can sound like a psych job that will not hold up when the real trouble arises. But older people who have gone before you and who have faced many of life's troubles know that every man has more strength, more endurance, and more intelligence than he is called on to use. In times of trouble, you dip into this strength and keep pulling out more until you are done with the problem and emerge victorious on the other side. Each time you do this, you discover a depth of strength you did not know you had. You also build more strength to face bigger challenges in the future. Eventually, you realize that being strong and bold in facing the world is a choice. You can choose fear or you can choose boldness. Inside, you have the ability to follow either path— it is a choice that you make at the beginning.

False Evidence Appearing Real

Most fears are just like the childhood monster under the bed. They can be terrifying. Your imagination can turn them into any size and shape. But you dare not look under the bed because they might get you.

Motivational speakers often say that FEAR stands for "False Evidence Appearing Real." Fear is a monster under the bed. It is not real. It is not the size and strength that you imagine. It is much smaller. It is much more afraid of you than you can imagine. Fear will run if you stand up to it and expose it.

Do not believe the "false evidence." Do not let a lie control and dominate your life, even if it is a lie that you created yourself.

Stop Thinking and Start Telling

Stop letting the fear movie in your brain define what might happen to you. Stop listening to the little scared voices fret about the world and what will happen to you if you dare pursue your dreams. Start telling your mind and your fears how the world will work. Use your positive beliefs and positive words to tell the story of success, accomplishment, and victory. This story needs to become the movie that you are watching in your brain. This needs to become the whispered soundtrack in your mind.

The victory story is just as real and just as possible as the fear story. There is no reason to prefer to listen to the fear story. It is based on ignorance and blindness, and it is not right. Create a story based on knowledge and an understanding of the world. Choose to prefer to hear and tell this story over the old fear story.

Tell your fears how ridiculous they are. Pick them apart. Find the flaws in their expectations of the future and bring those out into the light. Point out how long the fear story has existed, but in reality nothing like that has ever happened to you. Show your mind and your fears that they are a lie. Make them embarrassed to be taken seriously. Make the truth so clear to yourself that you would be embarrassed to seriously consider the fear story to be true.

Of all of the fear stories in your mind, how many of them have come true in other people's lives? List the people that you know that have been destroyed or damaged by the specific fear that is controlling you. How many of them can you count? How often have you seen the fear story play out?

Learn

Fear is a remnant from the ignorant caveman. The more ignorant we are, the more room there is for fear of the unknown. Cavemen feared the magical power of lightning and thunder, even though few if any saw the lightning strike a person. But they all trembled in fear of it. Their ignorance created a big hole in their mind, which was filled with fear.

Knowledge chases out fear. Knowledge and wisdom fill in that hole and make it impossible for fear to grow. Learning, education, experience, and wisdom reduce fear. Each of these is a bright light that we shine under the bed to show that the monster is not there. Knowledge replaces the unknown with the known. Knowledge is like a party of explorers going into the jungle to see and record what is really there. Exploration, observation, and learning show that no dragons or magical creatures exist in the jungles, the mountains, and the swamps. They are filled with plants, animals, and materials that are similar to those in our known world.

As you learn, you will begin to question your fears more closely. You will understand why they cannot be true. You will have a better explanation or expectation of the future—much better than the fearful expectation created by ignorance.

In an earlier chapter, we introduced the diagram that illustrates the supporting relationship among our four areas of success. Remember that one of these supports was the shift from stupid to smart. It will contribute to the shift from afraid to bold. Knowledge drives out fear.

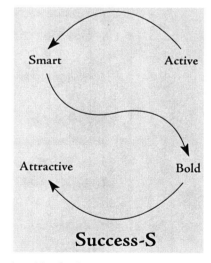

Success-S

Act Fearless

All of the steps above spoke to the fear in your mind. But this has to be translated into action. You have to move forward and be fearless at some point. Remember what Mark Twain said, "*Courage is resistance to fear, mastery of fear—not absence of fear.*" You have to choose to act fearlessly even though the fear still exists. You cannot wait for the fear to totally disappear before you take action. It will never be completely gone.

Choose a situation that you fear. Prepare an action plan, an attitude, words, or behaviors that are necessary to act in this situation. Charge into the situation using your bold new words and actions. Charge into the situation and learn what it is like to face your fears and to refuse to let them control you. Feel the exhilaration of being stronger than fear. Feel the victory of winning over your fear. Feel the strength that emerges when you are forced to be stronger than your fear. Show yourself and others that you have a new way to deal with the world. Show the world that you are bigger, stronger, and bolder than expected.

Then repeat it all again.

You will not get everything right the first time. You not perform flawlessly on your first try, or the second, or the third. But you will be stronger every time and, most importantly, you will see the evidence that you are stronger than you expected.

The unknown is now, *"How bold and strong can I really be?"* The unknown is not filled with fear. It is filled with strength that has yet to be uncovered and used.

Robert the Bruce is one of the great heroes of Scotland. He was the king of the Scots from 1306 to 1329. Legend has it

that during the Wars of Scottish Independence at the Battle
of Bannockburn in 1314, he was riding ahead of his Scottish
rebels against the English. An English knight spotted him,
lowered his lance and charged. Bruce sat firm in the saddle
without moving. Then at the last minute, he stood in his
stirrups, turned sideways as the lance flew past, and swung
his battle ax clean through the knight's helmet and head.
Was he afraid? Certainly. Did he show it? No. The effect of
these kinds of actions in the face of fear inspired his soldiers
and inflamed them to win the biggest victory in Scottish
history.

Stories of heroism in the face of danger and fear are inspi-
rational to entire countries. You can choose to join these
heroes by choosing to act fearlessly in every situation.

Disarming And Disolving Fear

Jonathan Davidson, author of *The Anxiety Book: Developing
strength in the face of fear* described a number of useful steps
for developing your strength against fear.

First, he says you must change your beliefs about yourself,
the world, and the situation. There is a short process for
changing your beliefs.

- *Slow Down*. Examine what you are thinking that is
  fearful. Make it clear exactly what you fear.

- *Write Down.* Explicitly write down your thoughts. Look for the chain of fear statements in these thoughts. Within that chain, find the one or two fears at the core of them all.
- *Throw Down.* Ask your fears if they can really happen. Force your mind to honestly evaluate the reality of these irrational fears.
- *Stand Up.* Tell your fears what will happen in the situation you imagine. Do not allow the fear to define the situation. Base your definition on the positive things that have happened to others. Your definition must be more real than the fearful thoughts.

Second, get some experience with the thing you fear. Expose yourself to it gradually and in increasing doses. Begin small. Build your confidence and your strength. Then take on larger situations. You may need a helper for some of them. A helper will encourage you to go ahead when your fear threatens to overcome your resolve and put you back into your previous position. But once you have succeeded, try it again without the helper. Eventually, you need to be able to face these situations without your coach, parent, or best friend at your side.

Third, create serenity skills. Learn to relax your mind and body. Learn to meditate and visualize the world that you want. You can control your thoughts in any situation. But you have to learn to control them when there is no threat before you can do the same under difficult conditions.

Forth, determine if you need medical assistance. Some fears and phobias come from chemical dynamics in your body. These cannot be changed through mental control and meditation. You may need professional medical treatment to change these chemical imbalances.

Fifth, create a healthy diet and exercise program. Diet and exercise also change the chemical balances in your body. There is no need to use strong medications if the problem can be solved through a healthier diet, taking vitamins, or engaging in regular exercise. All of these can change the levels of fear in your mind and the expression of that fear in your body.

Davidson recommends a diet that includes lean proteins like fish and chicken; whole foods like fruits, vegetables, and dairy; and controlled amounts of fats and sugars. This is the healthy diet that all doctors and government health departments have been promoting for decades.

Finally, use vitamin supplements to insure that you get sufficient amounts of the key vitamins and supporting trace elements that may be lacking from your diet.

These are the steps recommended by a medical doctor who specializes in managing fear. All of them are very manageable. Overcoming fear is not impossible. People use these steps to do it every day.

Paradoxical Intention

Victor Fankl was the psychologist who introduced the idea of paradoxical intentions. He encouraged patients to embrace their fears and to amplify them. In one example, a patient was afraid of sweating in public social situations. Frankl ordered him to consciously attempt to sweat more during social situations. The man's conscious attempt to do that which he feared broke through the grip that the fear had on him and made the fear seem comical and silly. This freed him from the fear.

Other therapists modified this idea and encouraged people to embrace the opposite behavior. In a situation, they recognize that a fearful event is about to take place. They identify their natural and habitual reaction to this event. They then consciously choose to do the opposite of that habitual behavior.

The attempt to control, change, and eliminate our fears is as ancient as the caveman. Today, it is a very active area in psychology and therapy. But it is also an active area in sales training, performance development, and athletic coaching. Fears run through every life and every activity. Every person has his or her own set of fears. But not everyone is controlled by their fears.

You will become a person who acts boldly in the face of their fears, just as millions of other people like you have done in the past and will choose to do so in the future.

10

Maintaining the New You

The world is very complex. Your brain has developed a number of techniques to help it deal with this complexity. One of those techniques is to create patterns of behavior, reaction, and categorization. Rather than evaluating every situation as if it were new and unique, your brain seeks to place it in a pattern that it has seen before. Once categorized as a member of this pattern, it selects behavior patterns that you have used in the past to fit these types of situations. Categorization, pattern recognition, and automatic response make it possible for you to do literally dozens of things simultaneously.

When you drive to work, you usually take the same path. In fact, if you analyzed this path, you would find that you probably use the very same lanes on the highway. You follow cars at the same distance and with a similar aggressiveness every day. You use your turn signal at the same distance from the intersection. You accomplish all of this without thinking about the drive. Inside the car, you may listen to the radio, think about your schedule for the day, remember the events of yesterday, use the cell phone, or talk with a passenger. You can do this because your brain executes parallel paths of action and because patterns allow you to put some actions on autopilot while you consciously think about something else.

These patterns or habits exist throughout your life. They are a big help in handling everyday routines. They are also a big hindrance when creating change. If you do not pay attention to your thoughts and actions, they will return to the old patterns that you have learned from years of experience. If you try to change as we describe in this book, your mental patterns will not always cooperate with those changes. Not at first.

Until your new behaviors have become ingrained patterns in your brain, you will need to exercise more conscious control over your daily activities than you are used to. During this period, you will be developing new patterns that will become your automatic responses in the future.

The following are some steps that you can take to insure that you remember to work on your new patterns rather than just repeating the old patterns.

Reset

Reset the world around you so that it supports the new way you plan to live in it. Some of these resets are one-time actions. Others need to be done daily until you are a changed person. We want you to reset your physical appearance, your social surroundings, and your mental attitudes.

Physical Reset

A physical reset is very straightforward. You need to change the way that you and your personal world look and work. We covered the basic areas that need simple physical resets in the prior chapter. These include your body, hair and clothing, home and office environments, and your car.

Social Reset

Change your social surroundings. Recreate the set of people that you live in and around. Part of the reason you have your specific personality trait is because of the people you associate with. We all tend to mimic the behaviors of those around us. Complementing this is the fact that part of the reason certain people are around us is the type of personality that we exhibit. It is self-reinforcing. We collect friends that mimic our personality, and we have a personality that mimics our friends.

As you become smart, active, attractive, and bold, put yourself into circles of people with these same traits. Your old circle is not going to shift with you. You are going to have to shift to new circles. This does not mean a total replacement of your friends and family. It means subtracting a few old relationships and adding a few new ones.

- *Change Surroundings.* Change the path you take to work. Change where you sit for lunch. Change your circle of colleagues whom you connect with at work. Put yourself in different places so that you will have the opportunity to connect with different people.

- *Work Relationships.* Every job has different cliques of people. Some are there to complain about everything.

Some work quietly and do not talk much about what they think or do. Some focus entirely on the world away from work. Some focus totally on work and "the hustle" to get things done. Which of these cliques are you part of? If one of these represents people who are stupid, lazy, ugly, and afraid, then that is the group that you need to exit from. Find the group with people who are smart, active, attractive, and bold and begin working your way into that group.

· *Boss Connection.* Almost everyone has a boss in the modern working world. Your boss is not the enemy. He is also not your buddy. His job is to ensure that some small part of the organization is working efficiently, legally, and productively. You are part of that system. and you need to have a relationship with your boss. You need to be able to talk to him and discuss the job, not just yours, but how the organization is working as a whole. Build an open, honest, and supportive relationship with your boss. Seek to help her do the job that she is charged with.

· *Recreational Circle.* Outside of work, become part of a recreational or social group that is smart, active, attractive, or bold. Smart may include people who take night classes. Active may include people who play sports or frequent the gym. Attractive may include people who volunteer their time at a shelter, church, school, or hospital. Bold may include people who are becoming public speakers. All around you are social activities designed to help you improve yourself, or that carry out activities that require the traits you are seeking to develop. Get involved with a group that has positive aspirations, not a group that is destructive to you and the world you are living in.

Mental Reset

Resetting your physical environment and your social environment are external activities. You can see and do certain things on the outside. But you must also make similar changes within your mind. Your thoughts and attitudes are the root from which most actions come. Your mind is also where your history and habits are stored. If you are going to make permanent changes to the life you live, you have to make permanent changes to the thoughts that you think.

Chapter 8 touched on the following methods that you can use to address your anger. You can also use them to take a mental rest.

- *Meditation and Prayer.* All societies have developed their own style of meditation or prayer. These are designed to take you out of the hustle of daily activity and let you focus on really important issues. Meditation with a religious root is prayer. In prayer, we seek to mentally and emotionally connect with a higher being and seek his guidance and assistance with life. In some societies, meditation is a means of bringing out inner wisdom. They believe that there is much more knowledge innately inside us than we naturally use every day. They seek to connect with what is already inside and improve life by bringing it out. Meditation and prayer will allow you to place deeply important things above the urgent demands of the world around you. It will also allow you to express clearly what you want for your life.

· *Affirmations*. In the last century, motivational speakers and writers have modernized the ancient practice of affirmations. In ancient times, chanting and mantras were used to reinforce patterns of thought in individuals and within groups. Today, this exists in two more structured forms. The first are verbal affirmations practiced daily. In these, you repeat statements like, *"I am not afraid of ..."* or *"I will be bold and confident when I meet with ..."* These may be used in front of a mirror or while driving. The second modern form is song. Church songs are messages to those who sing them and to those who hear them. They are verbal affirmations of belief and behavior that contain a musical pattern to make them more memorable. You can reset your mind by using verbal affirmations and song.

- *Listening.* Closely related to affirmations is the modern use of recorded books, speeches, and sermons. The cassette tape, CD, and digital player have become portable tools for learning and for mental reset. Millions of people use audio books and speeches to learn new information and to rewire the way they think. These fill up a great deal of empty time in which most people daydream or listen to popular music. They leverage inexpensive electronics to turn idle time into daily educational sessions.

- *Reading.* We live in a very electronically stimulated world. We are constantly surrounded by radios, televisions, digital music, and computers. As a result, we are the best educated generation that has ever lived on the planet. However, though these sources of information and entertainment are extremely educational, they are also rather shallow. Electronics make it easy to learn a little bit about everything in the world. But the best way to learn a great deal about any one subject is still the printed book. Books have carried knowledge for thousands of years and have evolved into a very effective form of conveying that knowledge to everyone in society. You need to spend time every day reading books. You may only have time for a page or two on some days. On other days, you may read ten or twenty pages. When you are digging into a subject that interests you, reading twenty pages is easy and enjoyable.

- *Ritual.* These mental resets must become a ritual in your life. You must develop a habit of doing each of them every day. They must become as habitual as brushing your teeth and eating. They should become something that you feel uncomfortable skipping, not something that you feel uncomfortable doing. Use your new scheduling tools to put these into your day and exercise your willpower to make sure that you do not squeeze them out. After a month, you will find them becoming comfortable and habitual.

Heroes And Helpers

Hero

The modern idea of a hero dates back to the ancient Greeks. Their heroes were demigods, people with one parent as human and one as a god. The ancients attributed the amazing powers of the demigod to a divine parentage. They assumed that really exceptional skills could only come from some divine origin. The demigod was also often used to cement the power of a king to rule over a nation. If the king had one divine parent, then he was chosen for his special position and all opponents were invalid because they lacked that divine origin.

Initially, these demigods all possessed special powers in battle. Over time, people with moral courage and strength became respected as heroes.

Today, we accept heroes in all walks of life. They are people who perform specific and valuable acts very well and who are worthy of emulation. They still emote the feeling of representing some divine good. They are a prototype for an ideal that is larger than an individual person.

As you become smart, active, attractive, and bold, you can benefit by having a hero to follow. The ideas that you are pursuing can be very vague and conceptual, without solid form or example. To put these ideas into practice, you may need to select a hero who personifies these traits and use him or her as a template for your own life and behavior. Your hero can be a flesh-and-blood person whom you see every day. If you have noble parents, relatives, or coworkers, you can find a hero in these people. Your hero may also live in books and movies. Religious figures are immortalized in inspired writings and present their principles and practices for millions of others to imitate. There are also biographies about great people and autobiographies by great people that provide instruction in specific ways of living.

Biographies are a popular form of literature precisely because they reveal the details of the life of people who are worthy of emulation. In America, the writings of George Washington, Thomas Jefferson, and Benjamin Franklin have always served as inspiration for the initiative, bravery, and intelligence characteristic of American independence.

I strongly recommend reading the *Autobiography of Benjamin Franklin*. This book is considered one of the first American "self-help" books, and it remains popular more than 200 years after Franklin wrote it. My own book, *In the Footsteps of Franklin*, extracts and distills the traits of Franklin that made him such a great part of early America and one of the first models of American success.

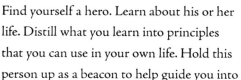

Find yourself a hero. Learn about his or her life. Distill what you learn into principles that you can use in your own life. Hold this person up as a beacon to help guide you into becoming the person you want to be.

Since this book deals with four specific traits—Smart, Active, Attractive, and Bold—we should point you to some people who are good examples of each of these traits. You should seek out overviews on each of these people, as in magazines, in Wikipedia, in television documentaries, and in book chapters. From these, you will find a few about whom you will want to read entire books.

Smart	Active	Attractive	Bold
Albert Einstein	Benjamin Franklin	Colin Powell	Teddy Roosevelt
Stephen Hawking	Lewis & Clark	George Washington	Harry Truman

Helper

A helper is your aid and conscience to becoming a better person. Pinocchio had his own little conscience named Jiminy Cricket. Many of us have a wife or husband who is happy to help us overcome our weaknesses and put on additional strengths. You may have a close friend whom you would trust with such responsibility.

However, recognize that a helper can be very difficult for some people to find and use. The changes we are talking about are often so personal and private that you cannot find anyone with whom you can entrust this kind of information. When it comes to things that are deeply important to us, many of us find that we are all alone. We live on an island with our own feelings, aspirations, and dreams, and cannot share these with anyone. This kind of privacy is not unusual or uncommon. Millions of people live on this internal island where their personal dreams remain private.

If you are one of these people, we will not encouraging you to open up to another person immediately. You will work on these traits alone. You will make more use of the Hero than the Helper. There is no reason that you should be less effective than other people.

We do encourage you to look around and start to think about who you know that could be trusted with this private information someday in the future. Do you have any acquaintances, friends, or relatives that you might trust some day?

If you do, then begin developing your relationship with them. Bring them closer. You can move very slowly. There is no rush. But we encourage you to do this because privacy with dreams and goals is usually characteristic of a loneliness of spirit. You probably find yourself internally alone with more things than just your dreams.

Talismans

In an earlier chapter, we mentioned the role that talismans have played in human life for centuries. Talismans, like heroes, are connections to a higher power or a higher ideal. They are a reminder of the dreams, goals, and expectations that you set for yourself.

Talismans originated as writings derived from the patterns of clouds in the sky. These shapes were believed to have been written by the Supreme Being. Later, these cloud writings were captured on amulets, weapons, and clothing. The amulets became the talisman and the words shared their power with the object. Today a talisman is often a special object, with or without special wording, but usually an object that has a special meaning in itself.

In ancient society, a talisman was believed to have its own magical powers. It was seen as having been instilled with the power or character of a god or some other powerful being. People believed that the talisman was actually acting directly in their life.

Sir James Douglas was a close friend of the great Scottish hero Robert the Bruce. After Bruce's death, Douglas took the heart from the body. He used it as a talisman to carry before his soldiers during their crusades in the Holy Land.

He believed that the heart of Robert the Bruce would bring the courage, leadership, and luck of Bruce himself to his contingent of crusaders.

Talismans appear repeatedly in fiction. As we discussed in an earlier chapter, *The Wizard of Oz* uses talismans. At the conclusion of the quest to defeat the Wicked Witch of the West, the Wizard bestows changes to the character traits of Dorothy's companions. He bestows these changes in the form of talismans. He gives them symbols of the traits that they seek and their faith in those symbols allows them to add that trait to their character. In the movie version of the story, the Scarecrow receives a diploma that symbolizes intelligence, the Tinman receives a ticking clock that symbolizes a warm and affectionate heart, and the Cowardly Lion receives a crown that symbolizes bravery. Each of these items is a talisman. They have no real power of their own. Rather, they are both an item of faith and a physical reminder of the trait they seek.

This is the real power of a talisman. The power comes from what we believe it can do and what we believe it represents. The power comes from inside the person who has the talisman and believes in it.

Today we recognize that ancient talismans do not have any power and we often refer to belief in talismans as superstition. Despite this, talismans are still very useful in all walks of life. They remain symbols that speak to our inner selves. They remind us to seek out a specific trait. They remind us that we are working on something special, not just going with the flow around us. As reminders, encouragement, and memories these talismans have the same power for us that they had for the ancients who believed in their mystical properties.

As you seek to become smart, active, attractive, and bold, we encourage you to use one or two talismans to remind yourself of your goals. These can separate you from your old ways and the flow of the people around you.

Christians wear a simple cross on a chain. Today, we do not believe that this symbol keeps away real evil spirits or vampires as ancient societies did. But they still remind us of who we are and who we are trying to be. They point to a hero that we are trying to emulate. They are a symbol of our being unique and different.

All kinds of talismans can be used in the same way to remind us to pursue a new trait and to be different than we have been in the past. They can be a big help in retraining ourselves to behave with boldness rather than fear, to use attractive words rather than ugly words, to engage in active behavior rather than laziness, and to use our intelligence rather than stupidity.

Talismans can be very personal or they can be something general. It is important that the talisman has meaning for you. I have adopted several talismans that are very personal to me. My younger brother died much too soon in life. While arranging his affairs, I came across a worn Swiss Army watch that he used for years. I picked it up and it has become a symbol of my connection to him and to the rest of my family. It reminds me of the good traits that he had and of the mistakes that I should not repeat.

Attached to my key ring is a carved Alaskan bear paw print that my wife brought back from one of her trips. This bear paw represents the boldness of the Alaskan polar bear, which is not afraid of anything on the tundra.

Historically, metal or wooden items that have been hand worked have made for very popular talismans. The weight of the metal conveys a solid decisiveness. The hand-working makes it unique and communicates the attention and intention of the message being communicated by the item.

You can look through your personal possessions and heirlooms for items that have special meaning to you, or to which you can assign meaning. You can also shop for such items in jewelry and craft shops. Your goal is not to find something that the seller says carries a message, but something in which you see the message you want to remember.

11

A Plan to Change

As we sum up the lessons of this book, we want to provide a straightforward checklist that you can use to begin your trip to smart, active, attractive, and bold traits in your life. These are some of the more powerful steps that you can take. In many cases, one step will contribute to two or more areas of improvement.

1. Add a multivitamin and vitamin C to your diet (Smart and Active). Start with any brand you find convenient. It is most important that you get into the habit of taking them every morning. You can worry about best quality once you have picked up this habit.

2. Exercise every day (Active and Attractive). Do anything that flexes muscles, bends joints, and circulates blood. Exercise until you perspire. Intensity is less important than consistency. Do enough that it takes away your stress and makes you feel vigorous.

3. Eat real food (Active and Attractive). Add food to your day that is original, whole, and identifiable as a single ingredient. These include vegetables, fruit, seeds, milk, and eggs. These are foods that have an ingredient list of exactly one thing.

4. Create a personal learning program (Smart and Bold). Begin to learn in the areas where you are weak and need improvement. Learn in the areas that your heart wants to pursue.

5.   Begin affirmative meditation (Attractive and Bold). The reset sessions change how you think about yourself, your life, other people, and the world. Affirmations in the mirror are one form. Silent reflective meditation is another. Prayer for thanksgiving and growth are a third. Positive diary keeping is a fourth.

6.   Cleans your life (Attractive and Bold). Clean your mind, body, and living space. Create an environment that makes you feel confident and proud. Create an environment that attracts other people to your spaces. Consult Feng Shui or other principles if you need guidance.

7.   Create a Hero Profile (Attractive and Bold). Write a profile of your behavior hero. Capture events and behavior that you want to mimic in your own life.

8.   Adopt a talisman of change (Smart, Active, Attractive, and Bold). Select a talisman that you will use during your affirmative meditation. Choose something that can go with you through the day. You will metaphorically draw your new self image from this talisman throughout the day.

9.   Write your life story as a hero (Attractive and Bold). Write your life history on a single page. Make it the story of a hero who rises above problems and solves

them. Write a second page on your future life history—you are the hero of this story.

10. Join a life building group (Smart, Active, Attractive, and Bold). Find a group that is working to make its members and the world a better place. Some people find this in religious groups, some in charities, some in hobby groups, and others in sports. It can be anything that propels you toward a better future.

11. Align your job and your heart (Active and Attractive). Your learning program will make you competent to do what your heart longs for. When you have the skills, move your job to align with your heart. Do what is important, invigorating, and enriching to you.

Those are a few basic and concrete steps that will get you started in building your strengths, banishing your weaknesses, and pursuing your dreams. Do not stop here. When you have these under control, add your own.

CHAPTER

12

Tools for Change

This chapter contains a number of the tools that we have introduced in the book. These are available for you to copy and use during your own self-evaluation and self-improvement practices.

Scale

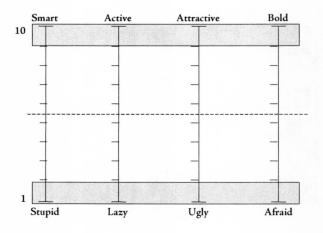

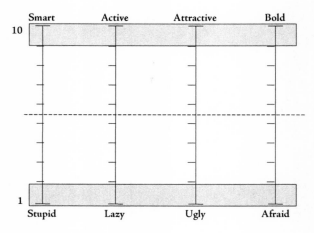

Schedule

	Monday	Tuesday	Wednesday	Thursday	Friday	Saturday	Sunday
6:00							
7:00							
8:00							
9:00							
10:00							
11:00							
12:00							
1:00							
2:00							
3:00							
4:00							
5:00							
6:00							
7:00							
8:00							
9:00							
10:00							
11:00							
12:00							

Milestone Chart

Event	Date:								
1)									
2)									
3)									
Milestone									

Goals

Goal	Category Smart, Attractive, Active, Bold	Description	Helper Who can help you get there?

Hero Profile

Name:

Short Bio:

Traits to Imitate:	Traits to Avoid:

Trait Transplant

Situation:	
Ugly Trait:	**Attractive Trait:**

Dr. Smith teaches workshops on
Overcoming the 4 Failures.
Please contact us to arrange one
for your organization.

Breinigsville, PA USA
26 October 2009
226492BV00001B/7/P